How to Raise a Jewish Dog

How to Raise a Jewish Dog

The Rabbis of Boca Raton
Theological Seminary

As Told to Ellis Weiner
and Barbara Davilman

Photographs by Susan Burnstine

LITTLE, BROWN AND COMPANY
New York Boston London

ALSO BY ELLIS WEINER AND BARBARA DAVILMAN

Yiddish with Dick and Jane

Yiddish with George and Laura

Little, Brown and Company
Hachette Book Group
1290 Avenue of the Americas, New York, NY 10104
littlebrown.com

First Edition: September 2007

Little, Brown and Company is a division of Hachette Book Group, Inc.
The Little, Brown name and logo are trademarks of Hachette Book Group, Inc.

The publisher is not responsible for websites (or their content) that are not owned by the publisher.

The information in this book is not intended to replace the services of actual dog trainers or actual rabbis. You are advised to consult with actual dog trainers for the training of actual dogs. Similarly, you are advised to consult with actual rabbis for actual religious training and spiritual guidance. Moreover, under no circumstances should you undertake to apply for rabbinical study at the Boca Raton Theological Seminary, which does not exist. This book is a work of humor, and the people, places, and animals in it are all used fictitiously. *How to Raise a Jewish Dog* is intended to do nothing but make you laugh. In the event that it is successful in this, we advise you to buy lots of copies and give them to all your friends who have dogs or had dogs, which, by our count, should be about 60 million people. So get started already. However, in the event that you do attempt to apply the techniques and advice herein to your own dog, and are unsatisfied with the results, you can't say we didn't warn you. Because we just did.

Library of Congress Cataloging-in-Publication Data
Weiner, Ellis.
How to raise a Jewish dog / by the rabbis of Boca Raton Theological Seminary, as told to Ellis Weiner and Barbara Davilman — 1st ed.
p. cm.

ISBN 978-0-316-15466-6
1. Dogs — Humor. 2. Dogs — Training — Humor. 3. Jews — Humor. I. Davilman, Barbara.
II. Title.
PN6231.D68W44 2007
818'.5402 — dc22   2007017915

20 19 18 17 16

LSC-C

Printed in the United States of America

Contents

IN LOVING MEMORY OF ALL THE DOGS
THAT HAVE BROUGHT US AND OUR FRIENDS
UNLIMITED JOY AND ABSOLUTE TSURIS

Sam

Ginger

Abby

Molly

Cassie

Matilda

Esa

Scout

Sweetie

Teddy

Lucky

Scamp

Frisky

Tucker

Abbey

Yeidle

Deedee

Thisbe

Hoochie

Cosi

Bigi

Teddy

Devon

Clarice

Zephyr

Foreword

They are scenarios familiar to anyone who has ever had a dog:

- You cry, "Sit!" to make your dog stop jumping and spinning so you can get the collar on him for a walk. But he doesn't sit. Instead he jumps and spins and frolics until you have to grab him. You do this four times a day for ten years (4 x 365 x 10 = 14,600 times), and he still doesn't get it.

- You yell, "Down!" when your dog plants her two front paws on the chest of a visitor to your home, as though asking for a dance. (Or, worse, she shoves her nose in the visitor's crotch.) But she doesn't get down. Instead she looks at you and wags her tail as though to say, "Some fun, huh?"

- You come home to find your dog cringing, his tail between his legs and looking as guilty as sin. It's just as you feared: he's rooted through the kitchen garbage can and scattered its contents as far as the living room. You rub his nose in it and cry, "Bad dog! No!" He looks contrite and apologetic. The next time you go out, he does it again.

- You're out doing the right thing, hiking with your dog. You take her off-leash because, what the hell, she loves it, and everybody else is doing it. She sees her friends and runs off. When you call after her, she pretends that she doesn't know you or — worse — that she's deaf. This continues to the point where you have to scream at the top of your lungs, "Who wants a cookie?!" so that every dog but yours comes running, and all the other dog owners look at you with disdain and pity because you can't control your own dog *even with cookies*.

People and dogs have lived in symbiosis from literally the beginning of civilization, and still, after 200,000 years, we can't keep the dog from jumping up on the dining room table and eating all the hamburger buns. We coax and scold and bribe and berate and threaten and praise. We're nice. We're not-nice. Nothing works. What can we do?

The Rabbis of the Boca Raton Theological Seminary have developed a technique that works, and they've (finally!) decided to share it with the world.

From purebreds to hybrids to mutts, from puppies to old-timers, literally any dog — and, just as important, any owner — can benefit from the Rabbis' program. It doesn't matter if you've tried other dog training plans or if this is your first one. And you don't have to be Jewish.

How did we meet the Rabbis and come to be involved with this project? That happened thanks to what at the time seemed like nothing more than a routine chain of circumstances:

Look familiar? Rabbi Monica feels the frustration and despair of many dog owners today. It is for them that this book was written.

Barbara's cousin's roommate's sister's boyfriend's therapist's mother had a pug named Sam. Sam went through the Rabbis' training and came out a changed dog. Word naturally filtered back, and we decided to see what this program was all about.

It has been our privilege to work with the small but dedicated group of clergymen-scholar dog trainers who have made the name "Boca" synonymous with canine obedience. We would like to thank Rabbi Paul, Rabbi Alan, Rabbi Monica, Rabbi Mark, and Rabbi Mary-Margaret, as well as all the other faculty and staff of the BRTS for their good humor, their deep dedication, and, above all, their abiding faith that the way to teach a dog to behave properly is to make sure it knows it will never be without you, and then to overwhelm it with love.

— *Ellis Weiner and Barbara Davilman*
Los Angeles

Introduction

The simple son asks, "What is all this?"
— EXCERPT FROM TRADITIONAL PASSOVER SEDER TEXT

We started the Boca Raton Theological Seminary (BRTS) in 1988 as an institution for the training of rabbis to serve the Reform-Progressive Trans-Diasporatic Neo-Revisionalist Jewish community. Our first facility, the northeast wing of the Forty Winkzzz Motel, had been closed for renovations for three years when we moved in. (We split the cost with the landlord to make the property usable and got a great deal.) Not only was our staff relatively small in number, consisting of two instructors and three assistants, it was also relatively young. Rabbi Paul, our founder and director, was at that time barely forty, and the other instructors were of course even younger.

In those days, no one lived on-site; everyone, both students and staff, went home at the end of the day. Even so, some of the faculty and staff, and a few students, revealed that they kept dogs as pets and fretted that the animals were unhappy in their masters' absence. Someone finally asked if it would be acceptable to bring dogs to the Seminary during classes.

Now, most theological seminaries discourage or forbid the

bringing of pets onto the premises because their presence has a tendency to distract students from their work. But we were — and still are! — young, and progressive, and constantly questing to find new ways to pursue old, traditional goals. We're always on the lookout for creative ways to be a Jew, new ways to be a rabbi, and new ways to train rabbis. So (with little understanding of what we were letting ourselves in for) we said yes.

And, in fact, it worked out very nicely. People brought their dogs in the morning and took them home at night without any negative effect on classes or discussion groups. We even began to believe that the presence of the animals had a positive influence on teachers, staff, and students. And, as will happen when people share important experiences together, we dog owners began to influence one another, to create a common culture.

We traded notes on training and feeding; we learned about exercising and communicating. We combined our knowledge, wisdom, and experience, focusing on techniques that worked and discarding those that didn't.

After a while it began to dawn on us that we were getting pretty good at this.

Inspired by our success, we began to "foster" dogs from the local animal shelter. We took them in, trained them, and "adopted them out" to loving homes for a modest fee. Thus, both the dogs and the Seminary benefited.

Indeed, the dog training program thrived to such an extent that we were able to purchase "the Forty" and refurbish it in accordance with our religious and residential requirements, thus expanding both our dog training and our religious instruction operation. The faculty and staff took up full-time residence in the facility. And then our students began to board there, too.

Rabbi Monica and Rabbi Alan at a recent poolside session. Note well-behaved dogs.

Not only were we learning and working together; we were now living together. But while in the classroom we were teachers, administrators, and students, at the dog run, or around the pool, we were all just dog owners teaching one another how best to train and care for these marvelous animals.

Soon word spread among the local Boca community that those crazy Rabbis at the BRTS had some skill with animals, and our neighbors — Jewish and Gentile alike — brought their dogs in for a consultation. And so, both to reinforce our bond with the community and to raise much-needed expansion funds, we began to offer dog training classes to the public. You didn't have to be studying for the rabbinate to bring in Rover or Fifi for a day's or a week's worth of classes. You just needed to be open to the unique form of training principles we found ourselves developing.

Our clients referred to it as "the Rabbis' Jewish Dog Training Technique." We simply referred to it as "the Program."

And we noticed a funny thing.

All the techniques we used in our dog training program came from two sources: the things our parents had done in raising us as children and the life strategies we acquired in response to our upbringing.

As soon as we made this discovery, we realized it made perfect sense because all of us at the Seminary were from essentially the same background: middle- or upper-middle-class assimilated Jewish American families. Our childhood experiences were quite similar; our parents' assumptions, their child rearing skills (or, as some said, their "so-called skills"), and the manner in which they related to us as children were almost identical. And the ways each of us adapted and responded to his or her childhood (through the use of psychotherapy, psychoanalysis, group therapy, antidepressants, and so on) were practically indistinguishable.

With so much in common — our personal histories, our outlook with regard to discipline and authority, our shared experiences concerning food, obedience, obligation, punishment, blame, betrayal, guilt, and all the other essential aspects of raising either a child or a dog — it was no wonder we were able to combine our insights into a single coherent, effective program.

This, then, became the Boca Raton Theological Seminary Program for Dog Training and Care. We offer it to our clients and, now, to the reading public because it *works*. Study its principles, follow its instructions, and the result will not only be a fairly obedient and reasonably well behaved dog, but also a very special bond between you and your pet.

We call it "the bond that lasts a lifetime — and beyond."

Chapter 1

Getting Started

The question we are most often asked by prospective clients interested in our Program is, "What do you mean by 'raising a Jewish dog,' and why would anyone want to do such a thing?"

It took us thirteen years of discussing and arguing and revising until we finally came up with an official answer to this that everyone at the Seminary could agree on.

How to Raise a Jewish Dog:
The Four Questions

1. Why is a Jewish dog different from all other dogs?

A Jewish dog has three important traits that an ordinary dog doesn't have: an exaggerated sense of his own wonderfulness, an exaggerated sense of his own shortcomings, and an extremely close relationship with his master.

2. All other dogs are praised when they are good. Why does a Jewish dog possess an exaggerated sense of his own wonderfulness?

A Jewish dog is not only praised when he is good, but he is praised *to other people* ("Look at what a good dog. Did you ever see such a good dog?"). This causes the dog to believe that he is good not only in his master's eyes, but in the eyes of the entire world. He thinks that *everybody* thinks that he is good.

A Jewish dog is also allowed to do things other dogs are not, such as eat table scraps, jump up on the good sofa, and sleep in the master's bed. These techniques — public praise and unconditional love and pampering — combine to bestow upon the dog a self-image of being excessively wonderful, which leads to the dog being happy.

3. All other dogs are scolded when they are bad. Why is a Jewish dog "guilted"?

The function of "guilting" is to make the Jewish dog feel doubly bad about misbehaving. He knows he has been bad, and he also knows that his badness has made the owner feel bad, which also makes him feel bad.

When he is bad, a Jewish dog is not only informed that his behavior may be bad in and of itself, or even possibly dangerous to his safety, but that his badness *harms the owner.* This explanation takes place in private ("You went through the garbage again? Why do you do this to me?") or in public ("I'm calling you and you're not coming? Fine. We'll stay here. I have nothing better to do and God forbid you should do anything for my convenience").

In addition to making the dog feel twice as bad as a non-Jewish dog would feel, this public scolding leads the dog to

Dog tragically out of touch with her feelings. We can only imagine her inner torment.

feel that *the whole world* sees what's going on — not only what a bad dog he is, but how thoughtless and hurtful he is to his master, who loves him so much.

4. All other dogs have relationships with their masters. What is so different and special about the Jewish dog's relationship with his (or hers)?

Traditional dog training programs call for the master to assert him- or herself as the "alpha," the dominant "dog" among the "pack," leading to a "boss-employee" or "parent-child" relationship between owner and dog.

We reject this approach for several reasons. First, we find it crude and unenlightened. In our opinion, it has led to a generation of dogs out of touch with their feelings, too eager to please the master and too afraid to explore their true potential.

Second, it leads to an obsession, on the part of the master,

After several months of our training, the same dog now gloriously in touch with her feelings

with obedience for its own sake. In our Program, we don't care so much about obedience or wielding power over the dog or bossing it around. We care about *solving problems.*

Third, the owner-as-alpha concept creates what to us is a very one-sided and, frankly, boring relationship, resulting in thousands of dogs being turned in to shelters and pounds each year because their owners find them incompatible or "untrainable."

Instead, we use a technique in which the owner and the dog *take turns* being the alpha — so much so that there are times in which no one is sure which is which! This keeps the relationship exciting, dramatic, and fresh — for everyone.

IT'S FOR YOU, BUT IS IT FOR YOUR DOG?

Once people understand the basic approach to raising a Jewish dog, their next question invariably is, "I like your system, but is it right for my particular kind of dog?"

Happily, after extensive study with literally hundreds of different kinds of dogs, we can give an unequivocal "yes" to this question. Our system will work with any dog, whether purebred, crossbreed, or "mutt."

PURE BREEDS

Each breed of dog has its distinctive traits. For example, if you throw a stick for a dog to fetch, the response you get will vary greatly depending on the breed of dog you're dealing with.

- A Labrador retriever will run after the stick, pick it up, and bring it back.

- A Rhodesian ridgeback will look at you as though to say, "Good. Now that your hand is free, you can use it to give me a biscuit."

- A fox terrier will spin around three times, jump up and down, and look at you as though to say, "You just threw that stick over there. That's so exciting! Now what are you going to do?"

Accordingly, while any breed can be raised Jewish, each one's special traits will be transformed in unique ways as a result of the training. The following table lists breeds recognized by the American Kennel Club, along with their primary characteristics and how they will be affected by our training program.

American Kennel Club Dog Breed Groups: Effects of Being Raised Jewish

Group	Breed	Characteristics	Effects of Being Raised Jewish
Working	Boxer, Doberman pinscher, Great Dane, Rottweiler, standard schnauzer, Saint Bernard, Alaskan malamute, mastiff, Akita	Bred for guarding homes and livestock and other jobs requiring stamina, strength, and intelligence	May "go into management" and "subcontract" guard jobs to other neighborhood dogs
Herding	Border collie, rough/smooth collie, German shepherd, Welsh corgi, Australian cattle dog, Australian shepherd	Large, brave, intelligent. Bred for herding, protecting livestock. Show quick response to obedience commands	Will change their technique, from "herding" to "directing," as for a Broadway show, resulting in happier, more talented, better-coordinated livestock
Sporting	Cocker spaniel, golden retriever, pointer, Irish setter, Labrador retriever, Weimaraner, Welsh springer spaniel, Chesapeake Bay retriever, Spinone Italiano	Bred for hunting, retrieving game birds. Types include setters and spaniels, pointers and retrievers.	Will think of birds not as "game" but as "poultry." Some may develop strict standards for how birds are killed.
Hound	Beagle, basset hound, dachshund, Rhodesian ridgeback, whippet, bloodhound, greyhound, saluki, borzoi, basenji	Bred for hunting mammals. Two types: scent (identify game by smell and either corner it or run it up a tree, then bark or bay until master arrives) and sight (identify game by sight and then chase it over long distances until it can be killed)	Possible improvement of hunting skills: scent hound may acquire advanced barking / baying technique and "talk" prey to death; sight hound may learn computer skills, track prey using GPS, Google Earth, etc.

Group	Breed	Characteristics	Effects of Being Raised Jewish
Terrier	Airedale, cairn, smooth-haired / wirehaired fox, Parson (Jack) Russell, Skye	Bred for hunting rodents and pests and digging after burrowing animals	With enhanced digging and burrowing skills, dog could become investigative journalist, private investigator, or, in extreme cases, personal litigation attorney.
Toy	Chihuahua, Maltese, pug, papillon, Peking-ese, Pomeranian, Shih Tzu	Bred for aristoc-racy, some literally as "lap dogs" to warm hands and laps of royalty in preindustrial eras	Expectation of being pampered will be unchanged but may show new interest in art, mu-sic, theater, etc.
Nonsporting	Bulldog, Dalma-tian, standard poodle, Schipperke	All other AKC-recognized breeds not otherwise classified	Nonworking dogs, after training, become especially well suited to intel-lectual, reflective pursuits, such as philosophy, theo-retical physics, etc.

MIXED BREEDS

Most dogs are mixed breeds or, yes, "mutts" — i.e., dogs whose ancestry includes a variety of different breeds (and different mutts). Now, it is no secret that in certain social circles mutts are held in somewhat lower esteem than purebreds. There may even be certain exclusive (or "restricted") kennels in which mutts are ever so subtly made to feel that they're not entirely welcome.

We deplore this kind of attitude, and it goes without saying that it has no place here at BRTS. When we encounter an owner with this sort of outlook, we remind him or her that "all mutts can be traced back to purebreds, and all of your precious purebreds can be traced back to — guess what? That's right. *Wolves.* So just let it go." Sometimes they do, and sometimes they don't, but what can you do? People are people.

In any case, all mutts are perfectly suitable for being raised Jewish.

CROSSBREEDS

In recent years a new technique has become popular — the deliberate crossbreeding of purebreds to create so-called designer dogs. The results of this procedure — in which the cherished traits of two different (and often highly disparate) breeds are blended into a single hybrid — can be delightful. Their names are, fittingly enough, formed by combining the names of the original parent dogs.

Some Common "Designer Dog" Crossbreeds		
Original Breeds	**New Crossbreed**	**Characteristics**
Labrador retriever, standard poodle	Labradoodle	A hypoallergenic assistance dog (still being refined)
Doberman pinscher, standard poodle	Doodleman pinscher or Doberdoodle	Slender muzzle, very athletic
Maltese, Pomeranian	Maltipom or Pomanee	Small, cute, sweet
Pug, beagle	Puggle	Sweet-tempered, intelligent, playful, social, affectionate
Cocker spaniel (American or English), standard poodle	Cockapoo	Highly intelligent, low-shedding, minimal dander, sweet-natured, patient, with a sturdy build

The preceding table shows only a few of the dozens of designer dogs now available. The column on the left lists the breeds of the hybrid's parents; in the center, the "portmanteau" name of the new offspring; and on the right, the hybrid's chief characteristics.

This "hybrid" trend has inspired certain graduates of our Program to experiment with the crossbreeding of three, four, or even more breeds, in the pursuit of a dog particularly suited to being raised Jewish. Bear in mind that the BRTS has no affiliation, either legal or financial, with these individuals. We do find their efforts to be of interest to the dog training community, however, and so their results appear in the following table. Again, the parent breeds are in the left-hand column, the name for the newly developed hybrid is in the center, and the hybrid's unique advantages for being raised Jewish are on the right.

New Crossbreeds Created Specifically to Be Raised Jewish

Breeds Used for Crossbreeding (AKC Official Name)	New Hybrid Name	Advantages for Being Raised Jewish
Saint Bernard, Alaskan malamute	Bernard malamute	Very literate dog
Soft-coated wheaten terrier, silky terrier, Kerry blue terrier, Welsh corgi (Cardigan)	Soft 'n' silky blue Cardigan	Respects clothes, looks good as an "accessory" when you dress up
Leonberger, golden retriever, berger des Pyrenees, Pekingese, Nova Scotia duck tolling dog, Spinone Italiano	Leon Goldberg's Peking duck Italiano	Cosmopolitan, sophisticated. Name sounds like kosher Chinese food with a Continental flair

(continued on next page)

(continued from previous page)

Breeds Used for Crossbreeding (AKC Official Name)	New Hybrid Name	Advantages for Being Raised Jewish
Havanese, Welsh corgi, Labrador retriever	Havane-gi-La	Lots of fun at weddings
Giant schnauzer, pointer, Japanese Chin, Black Russian terrier	Giant pointy-chinned Russian	Reminds many families of Eastern European ancestors
Siberian husky, Black-and-tan coonhound, Chinese crested, boxer	Husky black-and-tan crested boxer	Comfortable to have around you. Doesn't hurt circumcised men in the groin
Old English sheepdog, Staffordshire terrier, Chinese shar-pei, smooth fox terrier	Old English Staffordshire China fox	Precious, delicate. When displayed in living room, makes a nice impression on "company"
Gordon setter, Kerry blue terrier, Cavalier King Charles spaniel, Canaan dog, American water spaniel, pointers	Gordon and Kerry King's Canaan water pointers	Good guide dog. Familiar with seas and rivers of Israel
Standard schnauzer, Chart Polski, French bulldog, Shih Tzu	Standard Polski bullshih't	Good at negotiating with people from the Old Country
Great Pyrenees Labrador retriever (chocolate), soft-coated wheaten terrier, Alaskan malamute, American Eskimo, chow chow	Great chocolate-coated Alaskan Eskimo chow	Not a picky eater
German shepherd, Welsh springer spaniel, wirehaired pointing griffon, whippet, German longhaired pointer, giant schnauzer, bullmastiff, cocker spaniel, Doberman pinscher	Gerry Springer wire-whipping German longhaired giant stiff-cock pinscher	Naughty, ribald, uninhibited — the *Portnoy's Complaint* of dogs

We can't claim to have worked with all (or, indeed, any) of these fantastic new crossbreeds as of yet. We invite readers who own or know any of them personally to write to us here, at the Seminary, about their experiences with these extraordinary animals.

Now that you understand the basic goal of our system, and that virtually any dog will benefit from the training, it's time to talk about what we have come to discover is the most important part of the entire Program: the relationship between you and your dog.

Chapter 2

The Relationship Between You and Your Dog

The most important aspect of raising a Jewish dog is the *relationship between the owner and the dog.* We cannot stress this enough. Everything else — commands, obedience, rewards, and punishments — follows from this.

It is up to you, of course, to create and sustain that relationship. The dog, because it will want to please you unless it is one of those selfish good-for-nothings, will willingly collaborate with you. How, then, should you proceed?

WHAT IS HE (OR SHE) *THINKING?*

Every dog, like every human being, has a stream of consciousness running in his head during his every waking moment. We're not saying the dog is aware of it. But it's there nonetheless. It provides a sort of ongoing commentary on the animal's experience. We call it the Inner Monologue, and it changes as the dog's level of training changes.

By observing countless dogs, both in informal settings (at play, while eating, and in other situations when they do not know they are being studied) and in formal sessions (when they are asked an evolving series of weighted questions), we have been able to construct representative scripts of the Inner Monologues of various trained and untrained animals.

The first script represents the Inner Monologue of the untrained dog. We call this the Baseline Inner Monologue because it represents the mental life of every dog, regardless of breed. For the feral animal in the wild, it is the mental voice he will hear throughout his entire life. The more domesticated and trained a dog becomes, the more this baseline monologue will serve as a foundation upon which more elaborate monologues will be built.

BASELINE INNER MONOLOGUE: UNTRAINED DOG

FOOD! FOOD! PLAY PLAY PLAY. MUST GET SQUIRREL. SMELL. SMELL. SMELL. SMELL. SMELL. SMELL. DEAD THING! YIPPEEE! DEAD! MUST ROLL IN IT! ROLLING ROLLING ROLLING... AH. OTHER DOG!! SNIFF...SNIFF...SNIFFSNIFFSNIFFSNIFF OUCH! OKAY! SORRY! WAIT...PEE? PEE! WHOSE? SNIFF-SNIFFSNIFF...OH YEAH? TAKE THIS! AND THIS!...SMELL SMELL SMELL SMELL...RUNNING! RUNNING RUNNING RUNNING! STOP! WAIT. WHAT IS THAT? WHATISTHAT?? GET IT! GET IT GET IT GET IT GE— OH. TAIL. OKAY. FINE...SLEEP.

As you can see, the mental life of the untrained dog doesn't exactly provide much to "write home about." It is crude, impulsive, and unreflective. It displays only the most rudimentary sense of self and is concerned almost entirely with the most basic bodily functions and, sometimes, rolling around in dead things. This, then, is the given. It's the basic internal noise that

Typical behavior of untrained dog. Owner understandably becomes anxious about where guests will sit, among other things.

must be disrupted — in a nice way, of course — if training is to be successful.

Of course, each owner has his or her own Inner Monologue, too. The Inner Monologue of a typical (i.e., non-Jewish-raising) dog owner goes something like this:

BASIC INNER MONOLOGUE: CONVENTIONAL DOG OWNER

THIS ANIMAL IS CUTE/BEAUTIFUL/NOBLE/HANDSOME, BUT HIS INSTINCTS AND DESIRES ARE THOSE OF A "WILD ANI-MAL," WHICH ARE INCOMPATIBLE WITH LIFE WITHIN A HU-MAN HOUSEHOLD. THEREFORE I MUST — FOR THE DOG'S OWN GOOD AS WELL AS MY QUALITY OF LIFE — TEACH HIM WHICH BEHAVIORS ARE ACCEPTABLE AND WHICH ARE UNACCEPTABLE.

This is the mind-set of most owners when contemplating their new dog, more or less. Notice how its great sophistication and highly abstract quality differs sharply from the simple emotional directness of the untrained dog's Inner Monologue.

And that's the problem. Raising a Jewish dog (i.e., making use of our Program) requires creating a relationship between the owner and the dog *in which the owner and the dog learn to need each other so much that their Internal Monologues complement and reinforce each other.*

Of course, no one is talking about trying to get the mental life of the dog to be exactly like that of a human, or that the owner should try and turn into a dog. We simply mean that their two Internal Monologues should form an organic whole.

And, really, this is not such a strange idea, since the goal of even conventional dog training is the altering of the dog's Inner Monologue. Unfortunately, with conventional training, we end up with a blandly obedient robotlike creature without any snap or vim or verve. We get something like this:

Conventionally trained dog. Note complete absence of personality.

> ### INNER MONOLOGUE:
> ### CONVENTIONALLY TRAINED DOG
> I WILL SIT AND STAY AND COME AND HEEL AND DO EVERYTHING
> MY OWNER HAS TAUGHT ME BECAUSE I AM A GOOD DOG.

Frankly, about this kind of "training," the less said, the better.

OUR SYSTEM

So much for how we *don't* want the dog — or the owner — to be. What do we propose instead?

As previously mentioned, our system focuses on raising dogs the way we ourselves were raised as Jewish children and on the ways in which we reacted to that. First, then, the goal is to instill in the dog the assumptions and values our parents instilled in us. They include the following:

• The knowledge that we have to be perfect, or we'll be very disappointing to those who love us.

• The knowledge that we must be very careful whenever we leave home because the world is full of lunatics.

• The knowledge that most people are out to take advantage of us, so the only people we can really trust are our family.

• The knowledge that, no matter how smart we think we are, we are wrong about certain things, and the sooner we accept that fact, the better.

- The knowledge that we can be really very selfish and hurtful, so thank goodness there are people who are willing to put up with us, although God knows why.

- The knowledge that our hair will always look bad.

Obviously, some of these principles are too sophisticated to be adequately grasped by the dog. That's why we devoted several years to boiling them down into a small number of essential principles that can be efficiently conveyed to, and understood by, the canine mind. We call them the Four Essential Messages.

THE FOUR ESSENTIAL MESSAGES

For our training program to be successful, the dog must learn, and integrate into his view of you, himself, and the whole universe, the Four Essential Messages. They are:

Teaching the dog the Four Essential Messages. Note how Jax's expression shows his dawning comprehension.

Dog pondering the contradictions of the Four Essential Messages. You can practically watch the transformation of consciousness take place.

1. You are beautiful, intelligent, talented, and wonderful.
2. You are naive, unrealistic, and a fool.
3. No one will love you as much as I do.
4. When you die, they're going to have to bury me with you.

These four principles, like all basic axioms, are simple and powerful. Once the dog has absorbed them into his view of himself and of you, he will (whether he is conscious of it or not) begin to ask himself a series of important questions.

Your dog will wonder:

- If I'm so intelligent, why am I so naive?

- If I'm such a fool, how can I be so smart?

- If I'm such a fool, why does the owner love me so much?

- If the owner loves me so much, is it possible that she's telling me that I'm smart but I'm really not?

- What does the owner mean by "beautiful"? What does he mean by "talented"?

- If the owner loves me so much, why does she tell me I'm a fool?

- If the owner doesn't love me all that much, why is he telling me I'm so intelligent and talented and wonderful?

- If it will kill the owner if I die, does this mean I'm responsible for her?

These questions are important because once they start circulating in your dog's consciousness they will replace the more primitive thoughts with which the typical untrained (or poorly trained) dog is usually preoccupied.

However, in order to impart the Four Essential Messages to your dog, you will have to change your own Inner Monologue to that of an Owner Raising a Jewish Dog. It should be something like this:

INNER MONOLOGUE:
OWNER RAISING JEWISH DOG

YOU ARE SO CUTE I CAN'T STAND IT. DO YOU KNOW HOW CUTE YOU ARE? DO YOU? I JUST HAVE TO GIVE YOU THIS COOKIE. I JUST HAVE TO GIVE YOU THIS COOKIE BECAUSE YOU'RE SO

CUTE. WAIT, COME BACK. WHERE ARE YOU GOING WITH THAT COOKIE??? DO NOT BURY THAT COOKIE IN THE SOFA! DO NOT B— OH MY GOD, HE'S BURYING THE COOKIE IN THE SOFA. OH MY GOD, IS HE CUTE. DO YOU KNOW HOW CUTE YOU ARE??? NOW WHAT? YOU WANT ANOTHER COOKIE??? COME ON, LET'S GET YOU ANOTHER COOKIE. BUT YOU HAVE TO EAT IT. OKAY? PROMISE? HERE. WHAT'S THE MATTER? YOU DON'T LIKE IT? ARE YOU SICK? WAIT, I'LL GET YOU SOME ROAST BEEF. WILL YOU EAT THE ROAST BEEF? OKAY, GOOD. BUT YOUR NOSE ISN'T WET. SHOULD WE GO TO THE VET? LOOK AT ME. WHY AREN'T YOU WAGGING YOUR TAIL? WHERE ARE YOU GOING? COME BACK. WAIT. DO YOU STILL LOVE ME?

You can see that this Inner Monologue has several things in common with the Baseline Inner Monologue of the dog: It's primarily emotional. There are very few abstractions and a lot

"I love you so much, how am I supposed to go to work?" By the end of our Program, some owners are so bonded with their dogs that they have difficulty leaving the house.

Dog typically responds to overwhelming love by thinking, I love you, too, but go already. The mailman's coming and I have to get ready.

of urgency and joy and insecurity and pride and worrying about food and hysteria about health. Also note how it is directed not to the owner himself or to some hypothetical listener (like the Inner Monologue of the conventional owner), but *to the dog*.

An owner whose Inner Monologue resembles this one has learned, as we say at the Seminary, to "meet the dog halfway."

DEVELOPING YOUR INNER MONOLOGUE

Assuming your own Inner Monologue resembles that of the conventional owner more than that of the owner raising a Jewish dog, how are you to alter yours to suit our system?

Again, we must stress: You don't have to be Jewish, in either the religious or the cultural sense. You don't have to convert to Judaism, or study Jewish texts, or take any kind of formal Jewish instruction.

In fact, altering your Inner Monologue from whatever it now is to one more like the sample we've given you is fairly easy. All it takes is a few minutes every day, in the presence of your dog. The basic technique is as follows:

1. Stand or sit near the dog, at a distance of no more than two feet. The dog can be sleeping, eating, looking out the window, or engaged in any other activity in which he remains relatively stationary.
2. While staring fondly at the dog, say silently — to yourself, but verbatim, these explicit words — the following series of propositions, which we call the Ten-Point Cycle of Incipient Hysteria.

The Ten-Point Cycle of Incipient Hysteria

1. A dog is a miracle and having one is a blessing.
2. I can't believe how happy this dog makes me.
3. This is too good to last.
4. In fact, who am I kidding? It won't last.
5. It won't last because either something will happen to me or to the dog.
6. Either a disaster will take place or some crazy son of a bitch will come and do something horrible.
7. And even if the dog lives a long life, he'll probably get cancer. Would I do the chemo or just the radiation? Then there's the prednisone issue. And what if something happens to me? Who will take care of the dog? No one will love the dog as much as I do. The dog will die of a broken heart, just as I would if the dog himself died.
8. Why does it have to be this way? I'll tell you why. Because that's the way the world is.

Studying the Ten-Point Cycle of Incipient Hysteria. Dog (right) is perplexed by owner's behavior and wonders why brushing her teeth has become such an ordeal.

9. And don't talk to me about a heavenly reward afterward. There is no Heaven. This is it. This life is *it*.

10. That's why you have to value and embrace every possible source of happiness that comes your way. Like, for example, a dog.

Intone these propositions silently, in order, over and over, maybe while washing the dishes or brushing your teeth. You will notice that the last one leads smoothly back to the first. Make a photocopy of the Ten Points and keep it with you for ready reference. After a couple of days you won't even need it anymore; you'll have committed the propositions to memory.

After about a week you will notice that your feelings about the dog will have changed. Before this process, you may have regarded the dog with a combination of many different emotions such as affection, exasperation, amazement, annoyance, and love. Some you may have felt strongly, and some not so strongly. Now, however, you will notice that your feelings have grown fewer in number but greater in intensity.

And, as your feelings change, so will your thoughts. Your Inner Monologue will start to resemble the one of the owner raising a Jewish dog. Because, of course, that's what you'll be!

You will then be ready to master the techniques discussed in chapter 3, such as "Situational Martyrdom," "The It's-All-About-Me Spotlight Grab," and "Prolonged Being-Very-Disappointed-in-the-Dog."

___

Case History: Roxy

BY RABBI MARY-MARGARET

Roxy was a twenty-five-pound beagle-terrier mix that Lily saw running around the street in Simi Valley, California. Being an animal lover, Lily had stopped to help move the dog out of harm's way when another Good Samaritan gave her the dog's name and address. Lily was told that the dog was always escaping and that the owners either didn't care about the dog or were going through a rough time in their lives and were too overwhelmed to bother. Lily took the dog back to the house and rang the bell. "Is this your dog?" she asked. The man said "no" and slammed the door in her face. Lily had no choice but to take the dog home with her.

But Roxy, an alpha, was not particularly nice or friendly to the other dogs in Lily's world. So Lily decided to find Roxy another home. She searched, in vain, for three weeks. Finally, one day at work, Lily realized she was looking forward to going home and seeing Roxy. That was when she accepted the fact that Roxy was now her dog. Lily stopped off on her way home from work to get the dog an ID tag from the pet store.

But when she arrived home she discovered, to her horror, that Roxy had escaped. It took hours of frantic phone calling and walking to track her down.

Thus began one of the most endearing Jewish dog-owner relationships in the history of the BRTS, and the one that most completely embodied the Seminary's principle of Ultimate Ownership Martyrdom: "As soon as you commit to loving them completely, they leave."

THE DOG TRANSFORMED

Once you have transformed yourself (via your Inner Monologue), you will be ready to transform your dog from a wild animal into a Jewish dog, outwardly obedient, inwardly self-conscious and intelligent, and emotionally inseparable from its owner (you!). By the end of our training program, your dog's Inner Monologue will go something like this:

INNER MONOLOGUE: JEWISH DOG

WHAT'S WITH ALL THE *SQUEALING*? JUST TO GIVE ME A LOUSY COOKIE? ALWAYS WITH THE SQUEALING AND THE YELLING BEFORE GIVING ME A COOKIE. I NEED THIS? OKAY, I HAVE TO TAKE COOKIES WHEN THEY'RE OFFERED BECAUSE (A) THEY'RE FOOD, AND (B) SHE'LL STOP SQUEALING. EVEN IF I'M NOT HUNGRY I TAKE IT AND PUT IT IN THE SOFA FOR LATER. BECAUSE, LET'S FACE IT, I HAVE TO. FOOD. THIS MAKES HER SQUEAL AND YELL MORE (ABOUT THE SOFA) AND THEN — THIS IS SO TYPICAL — WHAT DOES SHE DO? SHE TRIES TO GIVE ME ANOTHER COOKIE. BUT I'M NOT HUNGRY! IS THAT SO HARD TO UNDERSTAND? SOMETIMES A DOG IS NOT HUNGRY

(ALTHOUGH I HAVE TO TAKE THE COOKIE ANYWAY BE-
CAUSE IT'S FOOD). AND SO I HAVE TO BURY THAT ONE IN
THE SOFA, TOO (MORE SQUEALING AND YELLING), AND
SUDDENLY IT'S THE VET! OR SHE BREAKS OUT THE ROAST
BEEF (EXCELLENT FOOD), WHICH, EVEN IF I'M NOT HUNGRY,
HOW CAN YOU TURN IT DOWN? YOU CAN'T. YOU CAN'T SAY
NO! TO ROAST BEEF. SO NOW I'M EVEN LESS HUNGRY THAN
NOT HUNGRY AND I HAVE TO LIE DOWN. MORE SQUEALING.
MORE "VET." MORE TOUCHING ON THE NOSE AND YELLING
AND SQUEALING. I'M NOT SICK, I'M FULL. BUT THAT MAKES
HER INSANE. I EAT, I DON'T EAT, IT DOESN'T MATTER. THERE'S
NO PLEASING HER. EVER.

Thus, the relationship between the Jewish dog and his owner is
entirely unlike the relationship (if you can even call it that) between conventional dog and owner. In a conventional relationship, the owner imposes his needs and desires upon the dog,
and the dog, within certain limits, alters his behavior in com-
pliance with the owner's desires. In the relationship between a
Jewish dog and his owner, the owner adores and badgers and
torments the dog. Then the dog adores and badgers and torments the owner.

Is there a name for this kind of relationship? There certainly
is. It's called love.

Chapter 3

Training and Obedience

OUR TRAINING METHOD: AN INTRODUCTION

Traditional methods of dog training involve using rewards and punishments to bribe or coerce the dog into doing what we want her to do, rather than what she wants to do. In time, the dog learns to anticipate the reward or the punishment, and behaves in ways she thinks will generate the former and prevent the latter.

Does it work? Sure — if you want to turn yourself into some kind of tyrant in order to teach your dog to be a robot.

We take a different approach. We don't train the dog that way because we don't believe in training.

Instead, we believe in *learning to work with the dog to solve problems.*

We teach the owner to use love and verbal communication, augmented by a variety of facial expressions, to establish a relationship with the dog in which:

- The owner teaches the dog what he or she wants of the dog.

- The dog teaches the owner what he (the dog) can or can't do or provide.

- The two work together to solve a given problem.

It may sound difficult and complicated, but it's really quite simple. Study the five-stage cycle that follows and note that everything you do with the dog, every interaction, from the most playful to the most exasperating, will come under one or another of its headings. We explain each stage in greater detail after the diagram.

Basic "Training" Procedure: The Five-Stage Cycle

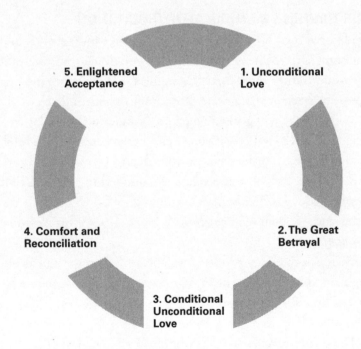

5. Enlightened Acceptance

1. Unconditional Love

4. Comfort and Reconciliation

2. The Great Betrayal

3. Conditional Unconditional Love

"Unconditional Love" (stage 1 of training cycle): Dog is pampered and adored.

Basic "Training" Procedure: What the Terms Mean

1. **Unconditional Love:** First, establish a preliminary bond with the dog with lavish, effusive love by doting on her, squealing over her, and the like. Deny her nothing, or pretend to deny her something and then "give in" and give it to her anyway. Be tickled and delighted by everything she does. This is the easiest and most intuitive step in the process, since it's the reason we have a dog in the first place. Be sure, when expressing this love, to announce it, not only to the dog, but to family, friends, relatives, neighbors, fellow dog walkers, and complete strangers, so long as the dog is present to witness it.

   Using a digital camera, take numerous photos of the dog. Document everything she does: sleeping, eating, playing, walking around the home, staring off into space. Send these photos, via cable modem or other high-speed broadband Internet connection, copiously annotated with your adoring comments, to all of your friends and relatives. If possible, set up a Web site or a blog, making the photos and commentary available to everyone on Earth.

2. **The Great Betrayal:** Now "training" begins. Teach the dog some command, either affirmative ("Sit when I say *sit*") or negative ("Do not jump onto the good sofa"). But be sure, when doing so, to *act as though the dog already knows everything she is supposed to be learning.* How? Through the use of attitude, vocal inflection, and certain effective words and phrases, which we will discuss. The idea is to convey to the dog that she already knows what you know because *the two of you are essentially the same creature.* In fact, at the Seminary we have a saying: "We never 'teach.' We *remind.*"

If the dog obeys, good for you. But she won't. When she doesn't, act stunned and incredulous as though you have been betrayed. Because you have.

"The Great Betrayal" (stage 2): Owner is stunned that the dog disobeys the please-get-off-the-chair command.

"Conditional Unconditional Love" (stage 3): Owner is devastated that the dog acts this way "after I've done nothing but love and adore you."

3. **Conditional Unconditional Love:** Tell the dog, and anyone within earshot, that you can't believe she's acting like this *after everything you've done for her.* Use such phrases as "this is the thanks I get" and "I don't know why I bother" and "why don't you just tear out my heart and eat it."

Ask the dog, "Why am I doing this? Why am I giving, giving, giving, if I'm getting nothing back?" The dog may look confusedly at you, as though to ask, "What happened to 'unconditional love'?" If so, administer the Preemptive Admonition and say, "Don't get smart with me."

Tell her, and any bystanders, that you are not punishing her for behaving badly "because that would be like punishing yourself." Instead, you are expressing deep disappointment in the fact that she is even capable of "treating you this way."

Explain, with exaggerated patience and "calm," that her not-sitting harms you because it makes you look like a bad master (or mistress) to the whole world. Her jumping on the good sofa harms you because, *as she well knows,* you've explicitly told her not to do it. Remember that, in this example, the object of the bad behavior — the entity that has suffered because of her badness — is not the sofa. It is you, the owner, who loves her so much.

Having done that, make sure that the dog and most, if not all, the dogs and owners in the vicinity are watching you, and then collapse, sobbing, in a heap.

We call this "guilting the dog." It alerts the dog to the fact that she has misbehaved and establishes the condition for stage 4.

Note: For milder forms of rebuke, see "Correction and Punishment," p. 56.

4. **Comfort and Reconciliation:** Remaining in a heap, stop sobbing and repeat the command or the lesson once more, but be sure to use the Tone of Exhausted Defeat. Instead of saying "Sit!" say, "So you really don't want to sit?" Rather than saying "Off the sofa! No!" say, with a sigh, "If it's so important for you to be on the sofa . . ."

Then, placing yourself up close to the dog, *allow her to comfort you.* This is an important part of the owner-dog relationship we mentioned earlier, in which now the dog has a turn at being the alpha.

And now you comfort the dog. Release her from guilt by saying to her *directly:*

a. "I know better than to react the way I just did."
b. "It's just that, as soon as something goes wrong, I go a little crazy! I start making demands and feeling betrayed and victimized. But at least I *know* that. I guess I'm still working on it."

"Comfort and Reconciliation" (stage 4): Dog, successfully "guilted," consoles owner.

c. "Anyway, I'm sorry for being insensitive to your feelings."

d. "I want you, and the world, to know that I'm more enlightened, more self-aware, and more evolved than that."

Then apologize to the dog and to everyone else in the vicinity.

5. **Enlightened Acceptance:** Give up and immediately undo or withdraw the command. If, for example, you've told her to sit so you can put on her leash, and she fails to do so, say, "Look, it's not that important," and put the leash on her while she's jumping around. If you've told her (a hundred times) not to eat the Kleenex in the bathroom wastebasket, but she insists on doing so, place the wastebasket up on the counter where she can't reach it. Bear in mind that the primary goal, in this stage of the training, is to solve the prob-

"Enlightened Acceptance" (stage 5): Owner and dog reach agreement to share chair regardless of how uncomfortable it is for both of them. Problem solved!

lem. The secondary goal is to not give yourself a migraine teaching the animal something it obviously is never going to learn.

Initiating this procedure will trigger a sequence of important effects.

Basic "Training" Procedure: Effects on Dog

- At first the dog will not know what she has done wrong.

- But she will assume she's done *something* wrong because "obviously" you love her, and you wouldn't act this way if she hadn't done anything wrong.

- The dog will not only blame herself for doing the wrong thing, but also for not even knowing what it is, or for not "remembering" that it is wrong.

- The dog will therefore feel not only in the wrong, but
  guilty. (Hence the term "guilting the dog.") She will fret
  that she's "not enough."

- This state of guilt can last anywhere from a few seconds to
  fifteen seconds. During this time, it is possible that the dog
  will learn the lesson.

- If the dog doesn't learn the lesson, you will have collabo-
  rated with her in fixing the problem in any case. And isn't
  that what's important? Because let's face it: life is too short
  to spend all day trying to teach a dog not to eat Kleenex, or
  whatever.

Note: Don't expect every lesson to conform to the Five-Stage
Cycle. There will be times, for example, when you'll be too
tired and/or irritated to progress beyond the self-pity at the
end of stage 3. There will also be times when you just don't
have the time or patience to do much more than follow stages
1 and 2 and, when the dog fails to obey, stage 5. This is perfectly acceptable. God forbid every interaction with the dog
shouldn't be a fully realized teaching and learning experience.
Don't worry about it.

COMMUNICATING WITH YOUR DOG
"Communicating" is a broad term and includes everything from
hugging and tickling, to using baby talk, to speaking actual
words and sentences to the dog, which is what we focus on.

Using Subtext
In raising a Jewish dog, it is essential to remember that everything you say must have a subtext. This term, taken from lit-

Rabbi Alan making small talk with dog to deliver subtext. Note how Alan's silly expression and idiotic manner mask explosive emotions, enormous pain, and other messages.

erature and drama, refers to the hidden or implicit meaning of anything that's said. Subtext is always conveyed *nonverbally*. For example, take two characters in a movie, eating lunch. One has just become angry with the other. The angry character, instead of saying "I'm mad at you" need only say "Pass the salt" in a specific way to convey his anger. "Pass the salt" is the text; I'm angry is the subtext, conveyed via facial expression, body language, and, most important, tone of voice.

Using subtext is important in raising a Jewish dog because that's how we convey the Four Essential Messages ("You're great"/"You're terrible"/"You need me"/"I'll die if you die") and, in this way, bind the dog to us and get him to do what we require (for his own good). In our training we emphasize conveying subtext using tone of voice. The table on the right shows some basic examples and includes the purpose (why we are speaking to the dog in the first place), the literal, verbal text (what we say out loud), the tone to use (how to say the text), and the subtext (what secondary message we are conveying nonverbally).

Basic Examples of Subtext and How to Deliver Them to the Dog

Purpose	Text	Tone	Subtext
Praise	"Good boy/girl!" "Who's a good girl/boy!?"	Qualified, tentative. Unresolved, with an implied "but"	"Don't get a swelled head. Nobody's perfect."
Mild rebuke	"No no . . ."	Gently chiding. Either slightly indulgent, or with a tone of reminding rather than berating	"Look, I don't really care that you did this. Life is short and I'm crazy about you. So ignore me. Just don't do it again."
Stern rebuke	"Bad!" "No!" "Bad girl/boy!"	Devastated, near despair	"How can you do this to me? What did I do to deserve this? Is it me? Is this my fault? Go on, you can tell me."
Neutral small talk	"So, tell me, how are you?" "Is everything all right?"	Stiffly "friendly." Obviously trying to conceal explosive emotions	"You have been bad, but I am giving you one last chance to acknowledge it and save me the heartache I can see is probably inevitable."
Brave reassurance	"I'm fine." "No, don't worry, it's nothing."	Neutral, flat, devoid of feeling	"What you have done is so unspeakable and such a violation of me (who only loves you and wants what's best for you) that I can't even talk about it."

Dog (left), confused by emptiness of small talk, wonders whether Rabbi Alan is having a stroke.

The purpose of the constant use of subtext is vital: The dog walks around in a confused state (which he blames on himself), wondering, What am I missing? What is the owner implying that I'm not getting? This makes him more susceptible to guilting.

Also, because he senses that your state is dependent on him, the more you express a subtext of despair or hysteria, the more he will begin to think, My owner is about to have a nervous breakdown. I had better stay close in case I have to alert the authorities.

Two Tactically Terrific Tones

Two other general tones of voice are especially useful. One involves making declarative statements in the form of sarcastic rhetorical questions. For example, the suggestion "Don't chew on the lamp cord. You'll get electrocuted" has about it a certain off-putting formality, not to mention a kind of bossy know-it-all attitude the dog can't help but resent. In contrast, the same recommendation can be conveyed by saying "So, you're looking for a way to give yourself a fatal shock?" But in this case the tone conveys not only a feeling of respect, but a certain jocular ease among equals.

In a similar way, a tone of world-weary concession can convert a message tinged with unpleasant anger into one the dog is more likely to want to hear — and thus, to heed. Rather than cry, in a fit of exasperation, "Fine! Tear up the bag of kibble and eat it all until you explode!" we recommend employing the word-to-the-wise tactfulness of "If you think you can fit that twenty-pound bag of kibble into your twenty-eight-pound body, don't let me stop you." This, too, is gently sarcastic, but also imparts a sense that you respect the dog's intelligence — and that you expect her to use it.

Useful Words

The actual words you employ when talking to the dog are extremely important. Certain words can imply a great deal, especially when used at the beginning of statements. Here are four exceptionally useful words rich in content:

So: Begin any command or question with "So." For example, "So sit!" "So who's a good girl?!" Use of "so" at the beginning of any sentence suggests that any comment, command, or question is merely the continuation of a single ongoing dialogue that never ends. This, in turn, means that you are invoking the entire past dialogue (not that it matters or that anyone can remember it), which enables you to put the dog on the spot with a vague sense of expectation. The dog will feel it's his turn to account for himself, which gives you added power over him.

(Note: Do not overuse this word, or the dog will start to assume that "So" is his name. If So *is* his name, pick another name.)

Nu: When you come home and the dog looks guilty, and you see she's been chewing and clawing her way through some nice throw pillows you just bought, the Yiddish term "nu" is a stronger, more demanding call for attention and accountability than "so." For example, "Nu, what the hell is this?" "Nu, what did you do?!" "Nu" conveys a more objective-seeming concern or distress than "so," and foists on the dog the obligation to "get with it" in ways that the rest of the world acknowledges. "Nu" is also useful to encourage the dog to "do his business" when you're outside and he seems to be taking an inordinate amount of time. For example, "Nu? Any time today."

What: An all-purpose introductory word and attention-getter, but mainly used to introduce a note of disagreement, skepticism, or incredulity. For example, "What, you not only have to eat that filthy-dirty Popsicle off the sidewalk, you have to eat the stick, too?" or "What, our neighbor Mr. Foster can't walk his nice standard poodle, Tucker, down the street without you making a big to-do with the barking?" "What" is an informal, semijocular term and should be used accordingly, to introduce rhetorical questions you don't really expect the dog to answer.

Okay?: Term of courtesy and respect, put at the end of almost every request, statement, or command so as not to damage the dog's self-esteem by appearing to be too bossy. Always include the interrogatory tone, as in, "Listen, Deuce, we're going out to dinner. We'll be back in, like, two hours, okay?" Saying "Okay?" even when you're not really expecting the dog either to consent ("Sure! Okay!") or refuse ("No! Not okay!"), shows the dog you don't take his obedience for granted and that you respect him as a "person," albeit of the dog kind.

Nonverbal Communication

Dogs are adept at reading nonverbal cues from humans — a phenomenon that is really not as mysterious as it sounds. Everyone is familiar with how dogs will respond to hand claps and whistles, for instance. Many dogs know that when an owner wordlessly holds out a leash, that means "it's time for a walk." A dog being raised Jewish is perfectly capable of understanding these cues, of course, but it is helpful for the owner to develop a broader nonverbal vocabulary.

Not that the dog will understand it, because he won't. That's the point. By addressing the dog in nonverbal gestures and signifiers, and having the dog either look blankly back in reply or ignore them altogether, the owner creates opportunities for

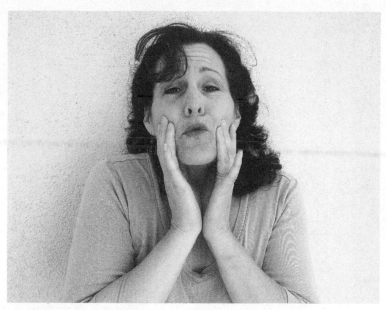

"Good dog! You are the best dog. I love you so much I can't stand it." (Note: To be delivered to dog only. Do not direct this gesture at a stranger.)

"Stop that now. We've talked about this. You know you're only doing it to provoke me."

"Time to go." Signals to dog several things: (a) that someone's shown up whom owner doesn't want to talk to, (b) one of those "troublemaking dogs" has arrived and the owner doesn't want to spend the day at the vet's, or (c) the owner has to pee.

"Bad dog!" Useful when you need to scold dog and don't want to make a scene.

"I give up. Do what you want." This tells dog that you don't know why you bother. Dog can also infer from this that he is the most selfish creature on earth, and that you only hope one day the dog has a dog of his own who treats him with the kind of disrespect and disobedience that he is showing you.

Situational Martyrdom (see "Correction and Punishment," p. 56).

Practice this series of gestures and expressions in a mirror until you can convey them to the dog smoothly and without hesitation. Note that, in the case of nonverbal communication, there is no effort at communicating subtext.

In each of these examples, the technique is the same: deliver the nonverbal message, confirm that it has not been understood by the dog, then sigh heavily, invoke stage 2 of the Basic "Training" Procedure ("The Great Betrayal"), and feel sorry for yourself.

COMMANDS: BASIC AND ADVANCED

With commands, we tell the dog what to do and what not to do and when to do or not do it.

Yes, it sounds harsh. And in conventional dog training programs, it often *is* harsh. In our program, however, this harshness is replaced by a sense of intimacy and comfort. To us, a command is a friendly reminder and proceeds from the basic premise that there are no boundaries between you and the dog. The two of you are essentially one organism, talking to itself, reminding itself of what it knows perfectly well it should do (or not do) and simply waiting to "get with it."

BASIC COMMANDS

It would be impossible to illustrate every command to the dog, since the specific circumstances of life are infinite. So we've focused on three absolutely essential commands that, if nothing else, will keep the dog under your control. They are "Sit," "Down," and "Come."

Of course, speaking to the dog is like speaking to a person: it's often possible and sometimes even necessary to say the same thing in different ways. That is why we have developed the Basic Commands in what we call the Five Modes.

The first three modes are "Casual," "Emphatic," and "Urgent." The Casual Mode conveys a command that, while to be taken seriously, is nonetheless meant in a spirit of easygoing calm. The Emphatic Mode asserts the master's authority and makes it clear that the command is an order, not a request. The Urgent Mode calls for immediate obedience.

Basic Commands: The Five Modes

	Casual	Emphatic	Urgent	Petulant	Hysterical
Sit!	"So you're going somewhere?"	"Nu, you're going to stand there all day?"	"What, would it kill you to sit down for one lousy second?"	"All right, fine. Don't sit. Stand." *(The owner then leaves the room.)* "All right, fine. Don't sit. *I'll* sit." *(Owner sits.)*	IF YOU DON'T SIT RIGHT THIS SECOND, I SWEAR TO GOD I'M NEVER GOING TO SPEAK TO YOU AGAIN, OKAY?
Down!	"What's with the jumping?"	"Were you told it was all right to jump up all over everybody?"	"Are you going to get down or am I talking to the wall?"	"Go ahead. Jump all you want. You always do." *(Owner leaves the room.)*	IF YOU DON'T GET DOWN RIGHT THIS SECOND, I SWEAR TO GOD I'M NEVER GOING TO SPEAK TO YOU AGAIN, OKAY?

(continued on next page)

(continued from previous page)

Come!	Casual	Emphatic	Urgent	Petulant	Hysterical
	"So, excuse me, if it's not too much trouble, could you come over here, please?"	"Nu, I'm waving for you to come over here for my health?"	"What, I'm here, you're all the way over there — and that's okay with you?"	"Look, you want to be over there, fine. I'm leaving." *(Owner leaves room.)*	IF YOU DON'T COME HERE RIGHT THIS SECOND, I SWEAR TO GOD I'M NEVER GOING TO SPEAK TO YOU AGAIN, OKAY?

"Casual" mode of commanding "Come!": Note how lightly ironic tone and elaborate courtesy respect dog's intelligence.

"Emphatic" mode: Tone is slightly sharper, not because dog would disobey, but on the off chance he didn't hear the first time.

"Urgent" mode: Use this type of command when dog hears you (because, believe us, he does) but you need to sell the gravity of the situation.

There is also a fourth mode, "Petulant," and a fifth called "Hysterical." The Petulant Mode is to be employed only after the first three have failed to elicit a satisfactory result. Hysterical is the mode of ultimatum and is to be followed by Situational Martyrdom and / or Complete, if Temporary, Despair.

"Petulant" mode: Essential for dealing with dogs who respond only to extreme sarcasm or who have abandonment issues. (Not shown: Owner turning and leaving)

"Hysterical" mode: Some dogs are easily bored and respond well when you throw in some theatrics with your commands.

IN PRAISE OF PRAISE

All dogs, like all people, need and deserve praise. Bestowing praise is not only how we show the dog we love him, but is a positive reinforcement to encourage him to repeat the praise-worthy behavior next time, assuming he can be bothered to listen.

Our method of praising our dogs differs slightly from other methods you may have seen or just naturally employ yourself. As

A QUESTION FROM ONE OF OUR CLIENTS

Q: I understand why there can be no subtext in the case of nonverbal communication, but are there any subtexts in the commands? Do I have to learn a different subtext for each of the Five Modes?

A: There *is* a subtext to each command, but fortunately it's the same for each one and for each of the Five Modes. No matter what the command, or what mode it is delivered in, the universal subtext is "not that you're going to." This subtext has a dual function: it not only helps create the optimum mood in which the owner can, if the opportunity arises, feel sorry for himself, but it "preguilts" the dog.

Practice saying this out loud the first few times you give a command (e.g., "Jaxon! Excuse me, if it's not too much trouble, could you come over here, please? *Not that you're going to . . .*"), and you'll see that it suits each one. Once you get a feel for how it applies to every possible command, you'll find yourself just naturally implying it from then on.

we mentioned earlier, one way we praise a dog is by delivering the praise, not to the dog himself, but to other people in the vicinity. This, as we said, encourages the dog to believe that the whole world cares when he is good — and, conversely, when he is bad.

Another important way of praising the dog consists in delivering the praise to the dog himself but making sure he remem-

"Isn't he wonderful?" Owner praises dog to total stranger. Note how stranger is thrilled and dog, believing entire world loves him, exudes self-confidence.

bers that *we* still remember that we are a martyr to his badness. We accomplish this by attaching a criticism of some bad thing the dog did either recently or, if need be, as far back as the beginning of time.

This technique reinforces the lessons that (a) the dog is not perfect and will always do something wrong, which means (b) he will always need us to show him the error of his ways, to forgive him for it, and then to act as though we don't care about it in the first place.

The accompanying table gives you some idea of how to deliver sincere praise to the dog while, at the same time, attaching an instructively deflating criticism.

How to Praise a Jewish Dog: Attaching Criticism

Praise	Attached Criticism
Who's a good girl and fetched the stick!	And I only had to ask her three times!
Good boy! You came right away!	And jumped all over me with your muddy paws!
Find the ball! Oh, very good! You found the ball!	Now if we can just "find" someone to fix that vase you broke last year . . .
Molly is such a good girl!	I can't believe you're the same Molly who jumped up and ate the steak off the kitchen counter last Wednesday.

THE REWARDS OF REWARDS

Normally, rewards such as dog biscuits ("cookies") and other snacks are given when the dog successfully obeys a command. We agree with this practice, as long as the reward is accompanied by either of the following:

The Not-So-Fast Qualifier: A remark, look, inflection, or other indicator that shatters the mood with worry and menace, suggesting that, no matter how good the dog is, it is capable at any moment of being bad. Recommended mood-shattering comments for giving the dog a cookie include "Here, don't get crumbs on the carpet," "Here, although you need the extra weight like I need a hole in the head," and "Here, now just don't eat it too fast and make me have to take you to the emergency room."

The It's-All-About-Me Spotlight Grab: An effusive display of admiration and praise grotesquely out of scale with the good act being rewarded. The goal is to shift everyone's attention to you even as you (ostensibly) direct yours to the dog. Your over-the-top praise (e.g., shouting, "Isn't this the BESTEST SMARTEST CUTEST DOG THAT EVER LIVED!?" after the dog has simply given you its paw) teaches the dog that, even when she does something right, it's your feelings that are important.

CORRECTION AND PUNISHMENT

Of course, not all training concerns getting the dog to perform certain actions. Half of what we want to teach the dog are behaviors we want to *prevent,* raising the somewhat controversial and uncomfortable subject of correction and punishment.

With conventional dog training, correction consists of relatively mild expressions of disapproval, including sharp verbal rebukes or "pops" with a leash. Punishments are more emphatic and can include a "cuff" under the chin or a "shakedown," administered by lifting the dog by the sides of the neck and shaking her back and forth while lowering her to the ground and delivering a firm verbal rebuke. (These last two punishments are recommended by our fellow clergymen, the monks of New Skete.)

We frankly don't care for all this popping and cuffing and shaking.

We have found physical punishments or correctives to be unnecessary when raising a Jewish dog, save for those occasions when some physical intervention is clearly necessary, such as removing the dog when it assumes an attack crouch vis-à-vis a nearby cat. Instead, we recommend what we call Situational Martyrdom, the case-by-case depiction of yourself as a well-meaning, unjustly abused victim of the dog's bad behavior.

Here are two kinds of infractions by the dog and their respective Situational Martyrdom responses.

Situational Martyrdom: "How can you do this to me?" This photograph captures the way posing rhetorical questions to dog forces him to think hard about what he's done.

Situational Martyrdom

For Milder Sorts of Misbehavior and Disobedience
The Unjustly Victimized Rhetorical Question: Say, in a voice choked with barely suppressed emotion, "How can you do this to me?" and just sit there and suffer.

The Ingrate Inventory: After prefacing with "This is the thanks I get," recite a list of the treats and luxuries you give the dog. Be sure to maintain a vocal tone that is oddly calm and devoid of emotion. For example, "This is the thanks I get for letting you chew up my good Thorlo socks *and* giving you an entire slice of pizza *and* letting you sleep in my bed even when [boyfriend / girlfriend] is over. Great. Just terrific."

The Existential Abandonment March: Say, in a clear, understandable tone, "Fine. Do what you want. I hope you have a nice life," and walk away, simulating complete abandonment. Do not look back until the dog comes after you.

For More Serious Infractions

The I-Blame-Myself Cry of Complete, if Temporary, Despair: Say, in a voice quavering with agony, "I can't do anything right. I'm a terrible owner and this is all my fault." Then run off, sobbing. The dog will follow. Allow yourself, with difficulty, to be soothed and assuaged.

The Inability-to-Face-the-World Coma: Retreat to your bed, get under the covers (fully clothed), and say, "I'm such a loser. I shouldn't be allowed to love something so much that I feel this much pain."

Prolonged Being-Very-Disappointed-in-the-Dog: Don't say anything. Don't even look at the dog. Deny that anything is wrong — to people who ask and, especially, to the dog. Just drag yourself through your daily routine until the dog shows he has the decency to feel bad.

ADVANCED COMMANDS

Once the dog has learned the three Basic Commands in the Five Modes, she is ready to be taught the Advanced Commands. Because they reflect a degree of complexity and sophistication not appropriate to the Basic Commands, we do not issue the Advanced Commands in the Five Modes. Believe us, one mode is enough with the Advanced.

We are continually revising and expanding the lexicon of Advanced Commands. For now, they include the following. They are to be issued in a clear, firm voice, while making eye contact with the dog so she knows you're speaking to her. You may, if you wish, preface each command with the dog's name.

Examples of Advanced Commands

- "Don't stare at Cousin Edith's hair when she comes over."

- "What do I want to eat?"

- "Don't mention the breakup."

- "I'm cold. Put on a sweater."

- "You don't have to call him 'doctor.' It's just a Ph.D. . . . In 'Media Studies.' "

- "I don't know how she lives with him. Tell me. How does she live with him?"

- "Israel? Please. Don't start."

Delivering the Advanced Command "I'm cold. Put on a sweater." Use this command only after the owner and dog have completely merged. Neither knows where one ends and the other begins. Neither possesses a distinct self. They are one unit.

- "If you want this painting after I'm gone, speak up. Because I'm not giving it to you-know-who."

- "We're going over to Mary Ellen's for dinner. Don't forget to eat first."

- "Milan is overrated. Don't bother."

- "If she starts talking about her son I'm going to have to kill myself and you're going to have to find your own way home."

Although it is often difficult to tell whether or not the dog is actually obeying such commands, don't be too concerned with that. The point of the Advanced Commands is to reinforce your bond with the dog by both sharing your personal opinions with her and by making her feel vaguely responsible for everything.

Chapter 4

Socializing Your Dog

So far we've talked about the relationship between you and your dog. But, as everyone knows, the world is full of other dogs and other owners. It's also full of people who, for whatever mysterious reason, do not even own a dog!

Given this fact, can anything be more important than preparing your dog for what he will find when he goes out into the world? Yes: preparing him for how he should behave because people will judge *you* based on the impression they get of him.

These two concerns bring us to:

THE FOUR KEY PRINCIPLES OF SOCIALIZING YOUR DOG

1. The dog should be carefully controlled and monitored at all times, so that he does not create a bad impression on other people, which they will transfer over to you.

2. While you're controlling everything the dog does, the dog should be encouraged to be himself and explore because

it's a big world with many wonders and discoveries and who cares what other people think?

3. Wonders and discoveries are terrific, but the dog should bear in mind that the world is full of dangers and diseases and lunatics that can strike at any second because life is not "fair."

4. While thinking about the dangers and lunatics, the dog should remember that he only lives once, so he shouldn't be shy. The dog should be instructed to be a doer, not a viewer.

These concepts, when applied appropriately, will result in a fully socialized Jewish dog.

THEY, THE JUDGE

Whether we like to admit it or not, our dogs are like our cars.

Just as there are people who judge us by what we drive, so are there other people who judge us by our dog — his appearance, his behavior, and so on. There are also people who don't care what kind of car we drive and who don't judge us based on that. These people judge us by the behavior of our children — which means they'll judge us, via our dog, in a similar way, if, as is often the case, we do not have children (and then they will judge us for not having children).

Our dog, then, is a combination car and child. People ask us, in our capacities both as dog experts and as rabbis, "What right do other people have to judge me, or my car, or my dog? They don't know what it's like to be me, just as I don't know what it's like to be *them*, and to drive around in *their* car with *their* dog and *their* children. So why should I care what they think?"

Our answer at such times is "You shouldn't, and you must." Society can be defined as the midpoint between everybody doing whatever he wants, and nobody doing anything. That is why we have ethical systems. Our task, as human beings, is to judge others as much or as little as we see fit, and then to go about our business.

What is the best way to teach your dog this important lesson?

We think it is by allowing him to observe you judging others yourself. We recommend this, *even if you are not a particularly judgmental person.* The point is for your dog to see judging in action and to get a feel for it.

Here are some suggested judgments for you to render upon other people as you walk your dog or sit outside with him. Be sure to express them in a clear, firm (but discreet) voice, so your dog is able to understand. If necessary, point with your finger to the person you're expressing an opinion about, but try not to let the person see you do it.

Judging Others: See It and Say It

What You See	What You Say to Your Dog
A woman in an exotic cape and/or turban	"Look at this one, the queen of Sheba."
A group of black teenage boys in hip-hop clothing	"Oy, these hoodlums with their pants. And would it kill them to tie their shoes?"
An old lady moving hesitantly with the aid of a walker	"Do me a favor. If I ever get that old, give me poison."
A man at least thirty years older than his wife.	"Some people have children, and some people marry them."
A teenage girl with a lot of body piercings	"Anything to cause your parents pain."

(continued on next page)

(continued from previous page)

What You See	What You Say to Your Dog
A group of nuns	"Why anyone would become a nun nowadays is beyond me."
A group of Japanese tourists	"Since when did we become a big destination for these people?"
Two lesbians	"It's bad enough they look like men. Do they have to dress like men? It makes it very confusing for the rest of us."
A teenage couple wheeling a stroller	"This is what happens when you stop teaching sex education in school because of the Bible or whatever."

"And what's their problem?" Rabbi Monica teaching a dog how to judge others — in this case, men doing weird martial arts exercises

Remember, you're not saying these things to get the dog to agree with you, since, of course, he can't. What's important is that he see how he will be judged by other people in a way similar to the way in which you judge them.

While your dog is learning that lesson, study the following table. It sets forth, in rather frank and unsparing terms, what various aspects of your dog's behavior and appearance "say" about you — or at least how they could be interpreted by others. Unfortunately, these hold true regardless of whether the dog is a purebred, crossbreed, or a "mutt." No one, and no dog, is exempt.

What Your Dog Says About You: Bad Impressions to Be Avoided		
Detail of Your Dog's Appearance or Behavior	Impression Created About What Kind of Owner You Are	Impression Created About What Kind of Person You Are
Too fat	Indulgent, indifferent to nutrition and health	You are a bad person.
Too thin	Irresponsible, lazy, cheap, indifferent to nutrition and health	You are a very bad person.
Nails too long	Slovenly, ignorant, stupid, horrible	You are a sloppy and, therefore, bad person.
Coat dirty and tangled, not properly groomed	Careless, untidy, don't take pride in dog	You are a crude, awful person.
Strains at leash	Lazy, uncaring about dog's health or his respect for you	You are an insensitive, miserable person.
Ignores you	Weak, negligent, reckless, indifferent to dog's safety	You are a spineless and really quite terrible person.

(continued on next page)

(continued from previous page)

Detail of Your Dog's Appearance or Behavior	Impression Created About What Kind of Owner You Are	Impression Created About What Kind of Person You Are
Eats off ground	Irresponsible, indifferent, ignorant about health and nature	You are a shockingly inept person in every respect.
Will go up to anyone	Naive, foolish, unaware of basic principles of safety and simple realities of human nature even a child knows	You are living in a dream world of pathetic fantasy and can barely be trusted to care for yourself, let alone your dog.
Will not go up to anyone	Tyrannical, overbearing, brutalizing	You are a hideous, almost indescribably monstrous person.
Doesn't wag tail, looks miserable	Oppressive, authoritarian	You are an insufferable bully and should be forbidden by law both to own any pet and to leave the house.
Too aggressive	Either grotesquely overindulgent or pathologically manipulative	You are a menace to society (animal, human) and should be under constant surveillance by armed guards, if not kept on 24-hour sedation in solitary confinement.

Obviously, then, it is in your interest, as well as the dog's, for you to instruct him on how to behave in public. Fittingly enough, the place and time to do this is not at home, but out in the world, surrounded by the very dogs and people judging you and whom you are judging.

These instructions should take the form of "suggestions" offered to the dog when you see him acting in a way that you think others might disapprove of. You should deliver them in a straightforward tone of voice, without sarcasm or subtext.

Here are a few sample suggestions that might prove helpful.

Socializing the Dog: "Suggestions" to Give the Dog in Public

- Sit up straight.
- Don't mumble when you bark.
- Don't look away when someone speaks to you.
- Don't whine. Either ask for something or be quiet.
- Cover your mouth when you sneeze. Don't wave your head around and spray everybody.
- Don't pull on the leash. It looks bad.
- Don't make me drag you. It looks bad.
- Don't wag your tail at everything. Not everything is so terrific.
- Stop looking so grim. Wag your tail a little.
- Don't sniff people's crotches. You didn't learn that from me.
- Be nice to people and they'll be nice to you.
- Don't be so nice to everyone. You never know who could turn out to be a lunatic.
- Don't roll in the decaying remains of dead squirrels. It isn't nice.
- Don't eat other dogs' poop. I didn't raise you that way.
- Can't you keep yourself clean? Cats do. Why can't you?

YOU, THE JURY

Once you have taught your dog the reality that other people will judge him (and, therefore, you) and that he should do everything he can to behave in ways that (according to you) other people will approve of, it will be time to teach him this:

Who cares what other people think? Most other people are either stupid or crazy. They can go to hell!

Both these lessons — heeding other people's judgments and not worrying about other people's judgments — are equally essential for raising a Jewish dog. They should receive equal emphasis in the dog's training. In fact, they should both be invoked and taught at the same time, on every occasion, about the same person or people.

Your goal, as always, is simultaneously to praise your dog and to take him down a notch, to give him the confidence to go out into the world while keeping him tied to you.

THE ENEMY WITHOUT: OTHER DOGS

Dogs are pack animals, which is another way of saying that your dog, no matter how intelligent and wonderful, will mindlessly follow the lead of some roughneck or hooligan if you give him

Beagle being a bad influence and teaching the others his bad ways

Bad Influences:
Undesirable Behaviors and Who's to Blame

Example of Your Dog's Undesirable Behavior	Probable Bad Influence	What to Say to Your Dog
Dog chews up sofa	Neighborhood mutt	"Who'd you learn that from? Your new 'friend,' Sparky?"
Dog snarls at another dog	Dog not being raised Jewish	"Oh, now we're bullying everybody? Acting just like those other dogs?"
Dog barks all day at nothing	Neurotic, "yappy" small dogs	"And where did you learn to bark like that? Because I'll tell you something — you didn't learn it in this house."
Dog steals food from kitchen table, counter, etc.	Beagle, fox terrier, other food-stealing dogs	"Oh, so this is what they teach you? Your so-called friends?"
Dog lies around all day, gets up to pee on floor, resumes lying around	Spoiled toy lapdogs — Maltese, papillon, etc.	"And I suppose this is what your fancy rich friends do. Well, guess what. We don't live like that."

half a chance. Of course we want our dog to have friends, and playmates, and to enjoy sharing his canine instincts. But what does he know about the proper kinds of friends to choose? Nothing, unless you help him.

How will you know your dog is "hanging with" the wrong kinds of friends? You'll know by his behavior. If he does anything bad, you'll know that it's due to the influence of his friends. You should reprimand him *immediately, at the time of the bad behavior,* and not just let it go for fear of making a fuss.

There are different ways of informing the dog that you know where he "picked up" the bad behavior. A sample table listing many types, along with the kinds of behavior that might prompt them, appears on the preceding page.

YOUR JEWISH-RAISED DOG IN A NON-JEWISH-RAISED-DOG WORLD

As your dog goes out into the world, he may find himself assuming that all dogs, like himself, have been raised Jewish. He will therefore assume that all dogs are rewarded as he is rewarded for certain behaviors, and are naturally forbidden to do the things he is forbidden to do.

When he discovers that this is not the case, he may become upset, disillusioned, and confused. He may question your Jewish training of him. He may want to know why, for example, he is allowed to eat leftover pizza crusts, while his friend Blanche is not. Or he may wonder why he is not allowed to sit on your lap when you're driving, whereas his friend Adelaide is allowed to sit on *her* master's lap in the driver's seat.

At such times, you should give him a two-part explanation:

- "Everyone does things their own way. Your dog friends who have not been raised Jewish have rules that are right for them, while you have rules that are right for you."

- "Look, this is how dogs who have not been raised Jewish are. And the same is true of their owners. These owners and dogs have different customs and beliefs. Sure, *we* think some of them are crazy. But that's how the world is. So get used to it."

Of course, your explanations needn't copy ours word for word. No matter how you choose to put them, what is important, as always, is that your two explanations be in direct conflict with each other and, as it were, cancel each other out. The first says that everyone is entitled to his own way of doing things; the second says that people who are different from you are crazy.

You'll know you've delivered these explanations properly if your dog's reaction is to squint, look puzzled, and then just walk away, shaking his head.

THE RISKS AND BENEFITS OF LIVING IN THE MODERN WORLD TODAY

Finally, a word about risk.

As we've already stressed, once your dog leaves the home he will be exposed to a certain amount of risk, whether from vehicular traffic, lunatics, fleas, crazy people, sinkholes, rabid possums, mailmen with a grudge, cyclists, careless Segway riders, falling icicles, foul weather, meteorites, escaped alligators, nasty children, and, of course, other dogs. You want to protect him from such threats, but you also want him to experience all, or at least some of all, that life has to offer.

How do you know when to intervene in a dangerous situation and when to let the dog work it out for himself?

Our rule of thumb is: Protect the dog from all human-based, possum-based, and alligator-based threats. In addition, be sure to become hysterical and drag your dog away from any other dog, cat, porcupine, gopher, skunk, or squirrel that appears the least bit hostile. Horses and coyotes are not even worth thinking about.

Despite every precaution, unfortunately, there may come a time when your dog ends up in a fight with another. Here is our standard formula with regard to intervening at such times:

Your Dog in a Fight with Another:
Steps to Take

- Summon dog by name. If that fails —
- Stand over fighting dogs and scream. If that fails —
- Grab your dog by scruff of neck and pull away from fight. If that fails —
- Look around for, scream at, owner of other dog. If that fails —
- Throw water on both dogs. If that fails —
- Throw water on owner of other dog. If that fails —
- Grab owner of other dog by scruff of neck and threaten lawsuit. If that fails —
- Grab your dog by scruff of neck, kick other dog, and drag your dog away, then return and kick owner of other dog.

Once Any of the Preceding Are Successful . . .

- Remove your dog from vicinity, check for injury.
- In case of minor injury, drive sobbing to vet.
- In case of major injury, drive in cold fury to vet.
- Sue, or threaten to sue and then settle with, owner of other dog.

By the time you have implemented these steps, either you will have succeeded in separating the contending dogs or the owner of the other dog will have broken up the fight. In either case, remember to implement the final four steps. Always check your dog for injuries, always drive to the vet either in hysterics or a white-hot implacable rage, and always sue, or threaten to sue, the other owner.

Chapter 5

Diet and Exercise

DIET

FOOD AND EATING

Many people "eat to live" (eat mainly to ensure their physical survival), while others "live to eat" (make food and eating a primary source of satisfaction and pleasure).

The same truism applies to dogs — some eat to live, while others live to eat. In raising a Jewish dog, however, you will confront a third practice.

A dog being raised Jewish *eats to live to eat*. That is, she eats to survive and then, once she has survived, she looks around and thinks, I like eating. What else is there to eat?

A dog raised Jewish not only combines the two rationales that humans have for eating, but also displays the two styles that humans — or, at least, Americans — use. Americans, as all the world knows, are both an extremely diet-conscious people and, at the same time, an extremely fat people. In fact, much of the time the reason so many of us are so determined to lose weight is so we can resume eating. Our national motto may officially be "E pluribus unum," but it might as well be "It's all about the food."

The more a dog is raised Jewish, the more he will display these two extremes of American eating styles. Sometimes he will eat as though he never intends to stop. At other times, he becomes quite picky and finicky. The owner of such a dog will have to learn to navigate between these two extremes. But bear in mind that, even when the dog seems the most hard to please and the most discriminating, he is probably just preparing for the time when he will resume eating everything not nailed down.

FEEDINGS: THE THREE METHODS

There are three basic methods for feeding a dog. Which one you select will be determined by three factors: the breed of your dog, the requirements of your lifestyle, and whether or not you are raising a Jewish dog.

1. Scheduled Feeding

RECOMMENDED FOR: Large dogs, dogs with big appetites
WHEN: Twice a day. Once in morning, once in evening
HOW: Set out bowl filled with food. Remove after reasonable period of time whether dog has eaten or not. If dog does not eat, do not put bowl out until next scheduled feeding time.
TRAINING BENEFIT: Teaches dog to eat at proper times; puts limits on how much dog may eat
LIFESTYLE BENEFIT: Coordinates dog's breakfast and dinner with human schedule

2. Free Feeding

RECOMMENDED FOR: Smaller dogs, dogs with limited appetites
WHEN: All day, all night

HOW: Leave full bowl of food out all day. Refill when empty.

TRAINING BENEFIT: Dog learns to self-feed, doesn't beg or whine for food

LIFESTYLE BENEFIT: Convenient for owners with unpredictable schedules, as food is always available for dog.

3. Dog-Being-Raised-Jewish Feeding

RECOMMENDED FOR: Dogs being raised Jewish

WHEN: Twice a day, plus all day and all night, plus at unpredictable intervals

HOW: Put out breakfast bowl first thing in morning. If dog sniffs and makes gagging sounds, prepare plate of scrambled

A typical weekday breakfast (on the weekends there's bacon). Note the human-type dishes, tray, and so on. Dogs think the food is better if it's coming from your plate.

eggs for him. If dog still doesn't eat, prepare turkey bacon and serve alongside eggs. If dog still doesn't eat, rush to vet. If dog does eat, allow him to finish, then put out large bowl filled with enough food to last entire day into evening. For dinner, put out dinner bowl. If dog refuses to eat, replace with steak, chops, chicken (boneless), meat loaf, turkey (boneless), and so on. If dog still doesn't eat, rush to vet. If dog does eat, put out large bowl filled with enough food to last through the night even though dog will probably be asleep most of the time. Also, during day and into night, give treats, "cookies," and so forth, intermittently and randomly. Also, at unpredictable intervals, leave surprise human food (uncooked steaks, hamburgers, just-arranged platter of chicken Kiev boneless breasts, bag of rolls) "on counter where dog can't reach it," then watch with secret pride as dog reaches, jumps up, grabs, and eats.

TRAINING BENEFIT: Encourages dog to eat, not only when hungry, but when happy, sad, frustrated, depressed, worried, celebratory, bereft, inspired, anxious, lonely, and bored. Also, because food, to a dog being raised Jewish, is synonymous with love, prevents dog being denied ready food *for even one second,* thus teaching dog that owner loves her. Surprise feeding helps dog exercise instinctual hunting-and-killing and sneaking-and-stealing skills.

LIFESTYLE BENEFIT: Scheduled Feeding allows dog to eat with owner, affords owner chance to discuss, over meal, with dog, the things Jewish people talk about when they eat, which is where they ate in the past and where they will eat in the future. Free Feeding allows owner to feel that she denies dog nothing, which is more than you could ever say about her parents. Surprise feeding allows owner to feel generous, robust, and in touch with "life."

Some dogs should not ever be exposed to Free Feeding and should be exposed to Dog-Being-Raised-Jewish Feeding only after extensive Jewish training because they are born "food-driven" and will, if left to their own devices, literally eat themselves into illness.

One such dog is Copper, a beagle, who proved an interesting specimen for our Inner Monologue study. What follows is a sample of his Inner Monologue before we accepted him into our program:

INNER MONOLOGUE: "COPPER" (BEAGLE, MALE)
Age 12

GIMME DAT FOOD. GIMME DAT FOOD.

Note: The full printout of Copper's raw Inner Monologue data continues with this text for twelve single-spaced pages.

Before enrolling in our Program, Copper's owner had switched his food from regular to low-fat. By the end of the training, the owner concluded that Jews and diets "don't work," switched him back to regular food, and remodeled her kitchen to include a single entrance with a lockable door. Cop-

Copper: "Gimme dat food."

per, meanwhile, learned a bit of patience from the Program and demonstrated a modified Inner Monologue in which the sentences were transformed into "WOULD IT KILL YOU TO GIMME DAT FOOD?"

NOT-EATING

Because food and eating play such a central role in the emotional life of the dog being raised Jewish, the subject of not-eating requires some discussion.

Not-eating occurs when the dog doesn't eat. This behavior can have several causes, one of which is that the dog is — supposedly — not hungry. However, since eating for the Jewish dog is connected with a variety of emotional states other than mere hunger, the owner is entitled to be skeptical when the dog professes that he is not hungry and to suspect that the dog is deliberately not eating for some other reason or purpose, including:

- Wanting to torment the owner
- Wanting to "get back at" the owner for some previous wrong
- Being in one of his "moods"
- Because nothing is ever good enough
- Because something is always the matter
- Because God forbid the owner's life should be easy
- Because the dog doesn't like the owner's cooking, apparently
- Because the dog thinks he's "fat," which is the owner's fault for giving him a poor self-image
- Because the owner stresses the dog out too much
- Or something.

Not-eating may be a sign that dog is sick — or, alternatively, that he thought he ordered the French toast. It is up to owner to figure out which. (Tip: One simple test is to make some French toast. If dog still doesn't eat, rush him to vet.)

In any case, the appropriate response to the sight of a dog not eating is to stand over the dog and say, "Since when are you not eating?" Continue to say this until the dog eats. If, after a reasonable period of time, the dog continues to not eat, say "Fine, do what you want" and walk away. Then feel guilty, return, and rush the dog to the vet.

DOG FOOD: COMMERCIAL

When raising a Jewish dog, what kind of food should you feed him?

The answer to this lies in the meaning of food, not for the dog, but for the owner. For the owner, food is the currency by which the dog expresses his love. That's why not-eating, as discussed above, sends so many troubling messages. When the dog doesn't eat, the owner takes it to mean: You don't love me.

Therefore we advise owners raising Jewish dogs to keep on hand, at all times, every possible kind of dog food, except for poison ones that contain wheat gluten from China. Be sure to stock "wet" (i.e., canned), dry, cheap, pricey, chicken, beef, lamb, fish, and every other flavor on the market. The idea is to provide the dog with every possible opportunity to eat. If (or, rather, when) the dog turns up his nose at one, try another, or three others.

DOG FOOD: HOMEMADE

A different strategy for feeding has been gaining popularity in recent years: preparing homemade dog food in one's own kitchen. We find this very exciting and encourage all owners at least to consider it, for these reasons:

The dog will eat better. Most people are capable of preparing food, in their own kitchens, that is more delicious and nutritious than commercial dog food.

You will look virtuous. When you make the dog's food yourself, you display to the dog, to yourself, and, most important, to the world, just how fully and selflessly you love the dog. How will the world know about this? It will be up to you to tell it. We have discovered that people who prepare their own dog food have little, if any, difficulty working that fact into any conversation with friends, relatives, neighbors, retail clerks, colleagues, complete strangers, and so forth.

You improve your ability to "train" the dog. By preparing the dog's food yourself, you raise the stakes of the dog's not-eating. You've gone to a lot of trouble. You've made something superior in every way — and probably far superior to the foods the dog's so-called friends are eating and which the dog thinks are so special when he happens to eat over at one of their houses.

Thus, when the dog doesn't eat the food that you yourself have prepared, he is easily guilted and made to feel that the significance and meaning of food, appetite, health, emotion, love, loyalty, obligation, and gratitude are all completely mixed up and inextricably combined. This is the perfect state in which he can be taught all the other lessons involved in being raised Jewish.

Of course, making his food yourself means accepting the responsibility, if the dog doesn't eat what you've prepared, to find out why. Is it the peas he doesn't like, or the carrots? Is it the parsley he finds objectionable, or the leeks? Is it the white mushrooms that put him off, or the portobellos? You'll have to employ a certain amount of scientific rigor and experiment by serving the same dish prepared seven or eight ways, each with a different ingredient removed, to find out what he doesn't like.

Be prepared to discover, when you finally do figure it out, that he's changed his mind and that you have to start all over again.

We know that most owners are busy people and that preparing dog food is not exactly near the top of their list of things to do. Still, we urge you to think about it. The Internet is full of recipes you can try when cooking for your dog. We also invite you to look for our book of dog food recipes — all tasty, easy to prepare, and with a Jewish flair — when it comes out next year, entitled *Try It, You'll Lick It*.

TABLE SCRAPS

The question of whether to feed the dog table scraps is a perennial source of controversy in the dog world.

Some say table scraps should be absolutely verboten, that human food spoils the dog's appetite for dog food and introduces sugar, fat, and other unhealthful ingredients into the animal's diet. Add to this the well-known dangers of chocolate and, some believe, tomatoes, and the perils of sharp bones that can splinter.

Others believe that table scraps, when selected and doled out judiciously, are harmless treats that please the dog and strengthen her affection for the owner.

With regard to raising a Jewish dog, we have decided we are comfortable with the latter position, with an important qualification. First, though, we must reiterate: never give the dog anything chemically or physically dangerous.

That being said, we advise that the presentation of a safe, modest portion of table scraps be accompanied by the appropriate verbal instruction, as set forth in the following table:

"This is excellent lox, so I hope you appreciate it, although I'm sure you don't."
Criticizing dog while giving him a special treat is for his own good.

What to Say When Serving Table Scraps

Type of Table Scrap	Verbal Instruction
Meat, poultry (boneless)	"See how nice? From my own plate!"
Fish, shellfish	"[Name of seafood] is my favorite, so I hope you appreciate it."
Potato, rice, pasta	"No, no, you enjoy it. I'll have a piece of bread."
Vegetables	"You think [Bessie / Scout / Dizzy] eats this well? I doubt it."
Bread, roll, bagel, pizza crust, etc.	"I don't know why I'm giving you this. It freezes very well."
Eggs	"Of course I like it! But I'll be all right . . ."

WATER

Water is of course necessary for life itself, and normal dogs should have available to them, at all times, a bowl of clean drinking water. It is usually placed on the floor in the kitchen beside the dog's food bowl.

We recommend, for a dog being raised Jewish, that you leave a bowl of clean drinking water on the floor of every room in the house, as well as in the larger or most-trafficked hallways. True, your dog, if he is in another room of the house, is perfectly capable of traveling to the kitchen to drink water. But thank God he doesn't have to! Why should your dog have to walk a long way to get precious, life-sustaining water?

OVERFEEDING

As you would expect in a country obsessed with both eating and dieting, there is an ongoing debate in the United States over the question "What is overfeeding?" Should a dog be allowed to eat all she wants, on the assumption that she must still be hungry? Or does every dog have an optimum weight, mandating that the owner protect her from recreational (or, worse, neurotic) overeating?

We find ourselves somewhere in the middle of this controversy. Our policy is: Don't overfeed the dog. Still, if you do, is that so bad? At least the dog isn't skin and bones, which people notice and which creates a bad impression.

EXERCISE

It is essential, in raising a Jewish dog, that the dog and owner do absolutely everything possible together: eating, sleeping, socializing, and, yes, exercising.

Interestingly, people and dogs approach exercise from two different angles. Most people exercise because they feel they have to; dogs exercise because they want to. Even lazy, indolent dogs who don't particularly want to exercise are happy to go for a walk, which provides them with opportunities to smell new things. And who is to say that smelling new things isn't, in some wonderful and mysterious way, a form of canine exercise? Not us!

Then again, not all human forms of exercise are appropriate for the dog. Consult the following table to see what kinds of workouts will "work."

Exercising with Your Dog: Good and Bad Examples		
Exercise	**Appropriate for Your Dog?**	**Comment**
Jogging	Yes	Keep comfortable pace for dog; resist temptation to take dog's pulse
Hiking	Yes	Special equipment required; see "Exercise Apparel and Equipment," p. 86
Walking	Yes	Maintain brisk pace; strolling, window-shopping, shpotziring, or shmying do not count as exercise either for you or dog.
Yoga	No	Strange positions (asanas) are frightening, provoking, to dog.
Free weights	No	Dog lacks opposable thumbs, cannot lift barbells. Clanking weights frightening to dog's sensitive hearing

(continued on next page)

(continued from previous page)

Exercise	Appropriate for Your Dog?	Comment
Weight machines, Nautilus, etc.	No	Dog does not need tight abs, firm glutes, or "definition."
Bicycling — dog rides own bike	No	Dog cannot ride bike. (Cannot ride tricycle either)
Bicycling — dog runs alongside bike on leash	No	Normal bike speed exhausting to dog; slower speed causes bike to "stall," fall over onto dog, litigious pedestrian, etc.
Pilates	No	Whole thing too weird for dog to be part of
Martial arts (judo, jujitsu, tae kwon do, tae bo, krav maga, kung fu, tang soo do, hwa rang do, capoeira, etc.)	No	Loud martial arts shouts disorient, frighten, dog. Dog will attack teacher and other students who "menace" owner

EXERCISE APPAREL AND EQUIPMENT

In general, by exercising we mean hiking or walking — and not, therefore, "playing" in the relatively safe confines of a dog run or other, similar kind of park. Exercise is a prolonged activity that, by definition, takes you and the dog away from the security of the home and into unfamiliar neighborhoods or city streets, canyons, fields, forests, beaches, highways, and other potentially dangerous places.

For this reason, because it's better to be safe than sorry and you never know what kind of lunatics are out there, we suggest the following equipment as a bare minimum for exercising.

Working out with a Pilates ball is not appropriate for dogs. As for the Pilates benches with the mats and the weights and the pulleys, don't even go there.

Minimum Necessities for Exercising a Dog Being Raised Jewish

- First aid kit: In case of falls, scrapes, attacks by coyotes or other dogs, etc.
- Bottled water: One for you, one for dog. Better yet, two for each.
- Benadryl: For snakebites, allergies (the dog's), poison ivy, etc.
- Material or a sweatshirt: For fashioning a sling, "sledge," stretcher, or other device for physically transporting dog in case of injury, or if it just gets too tired to walk anymore, or if it's too hot
- Cell phone: For summoning police, fire, EMTs, helicopters, coast guard, etc., in case of emergencies
- Camera feature in cell phone: For taking photos of how cute dog is so you don't forget

- Swiss Army knife (10-blade minimum): For all-around survival needs
- Flare: For nighttime emergencies
- Crossword puzzle/book/iPod: To pass time while waiting for dog to come back
- Can of Mace: For warding off hoodlums, other (nasty) dogs and/or their owners
- Mini-bullhorn: To call dog after she runs off in search of God knows what
- Whistle: See Mini-bullhorn
- Squeaky toy: To lure dog back once she is in sight
- Snacks and cookies: To lure dog back
- Snacks and cookies for other dogs: To lure your dog back by showing her that other dogs are having a great time getting snacks from you
- GPS tracking device: To avoid getting lost
- Tissues: To wipe away tears after dog "runs away forever," until she comes back
- Sunblock: In case looking for dog requires you to leave shaded area
- Flashlight: For nighttime emergencies and for reading book
- Extra sweater: For you, after sundown
- Extra sweater: For dog
- Preprinted lost dog posters (laminated): Should include name and nicknames; photo of dog; general description of her appearance; favorite foods, favorite toys, favorite movies, favorite color, etc.; and your cell, home, work, neighbor's, mother's, therapist's, and attorney's phone numbers
- Tape/hammer and nails/tacks/pushpins: For mounting poster

Owner with absolute minimum necessities for hiking with dog.
(Not shown: bullhorn, sunglasses, rain poncho, paperback book in backpack,
wagon or stroller, deli platter for rescue workers who help find dog)

- Deli platter (at home): To reward search parties who help you find lost dog
- Wagon or stroller: For others to transport you (while holding dog) back home if both of you are injured, too tired, or it's too hot

FALSE EXERCISE

Some activities, however strenuous, cannot rightly be construed as exercise, and should not be considered adequate substitutes for an actual walk. They include:

- Running from window to window barking at mailman
- Running around trying to bury bone/cookie
- Jumping up and down when you are putting on leash
- Pacing along with you as you talk to your mother on phone
- Jumping into your suitcase as you pack for a trip
- Pawing the front door when he hears you arriving
- Barking at doorbells or door knocks on television

ON-LEASH VERSUS OFF-LEASH

Most dogs love being off-leash. While many walkers will encourage the leashed dog to move at whatever brisk pace she wants, and will gamely try to keep up, nothing can compare with the unfettered zeal with which most dogs trot and run once the leash is removed.

The owner of a Jewish dog therefore faces a difficult choice. On the one hand, she wishes to indulge the dog's desire to run and play. On the other, she wants to protect the dog from all the dangers in the world — real, potential, and imagined — by not allowing him to stray more than fifteen feet in any direction.

We say it is acceptable, in an enclosed area such as a dog park or dog run, to remove the leash and allow the dog to run free. Just make sure he runs and plays with non-Jewish dogs, who will respond quickly when their owners call them in case of danger, trouble, or the appearance of lunatics about to do God-knows-what. Your dog will follow those dogs to their owners, where you may put the leash back on and get back to your normal lives.

Chapter 6

Basic Equipment

The basic equipment necessary for raising a Jewish dog is somewhat different from the basic equipment needed for raising a conventional dog.

With a conventionally raised dog, equipment is mainly utilitarian. You buy things for their intended use, and if you or the dog doesn't "need" it, you don't buy it.

When raising a Jewish dog, however, your goal is more ambitious. You still have need of the usual dog-related items such as collars, leashes, and bowls. But bear in mind that you're buying equipment not just to accomplish workaday tasks, but to create, mold, and enhance your relationship with the dog.

AN IMPORTANT PHRASE

One phrase you will find particularly useful when giving something to the dog, and then watching as he either doesn't like it or stops liking it, is "It's never enough."

Practice saying this phrase out loud ("It's NEH-ver e-NUFF," with the first syllable of "never" receiving the most emphasis), either to yourself, to the dog, or to other people and/or their dogs, until you can repeat it with a combination of fatalism and resignation.

When you say it, this is what you are communicating via subtext: I give the dog all these things that he wants, or that he should want, or that I would want if I were a dog, and he still wants other things. This is abusive to me, but I will endure it without complaint because of how selflessly I love the dog.

Obviously, this is a key phrase for invoking Situational Martyrdom (see page 57). It can also function as a sort of an introductory throat-clearing warm-up for guilting the dog. (For example, "How can you not like these? They're *cheese-flavored plastic squirrels*! Man, it's never enough, is it?" Pause. "Do you know how much these things cost? Plus shipping?")

The "It's never enough" phrase is essential as you become adept at pampering the dog.

INTRODUCTION TO PAMPERING

As we explain in chapter 3, the first stage of our Basic "Training" Procedure calls for "Unconditional Love." How do you display such love? First, of course, in the usual physical and emotional ways: hugging, petting, scratching, tickling, baby-talking, and all the other ways you express the fact that you're just crazy about your dog.

You also, naturally, will want to provide the physical necessities for the dog's survival and good health, including food, water, a place to sleep, and so forth.

And then there's pampering.

For most owners, pampering involves giving the dog luxuries, bonuses, accessories, extras, presents, special rewards, a-little-somethings, and everything else above and beyond the necessities. But when you're raising a Jewish dog, pampering is not something you do on a whim or because you're in a good mood or because the dog has done something special.

When raising a Jewish dog, pampering *is* a necessity.

And there are many different ways to do it. That's why we have devised what we call "The Six-Pointed Mogen David Star of Pampering." It illustrates the six basic (and different) ways to pamper your dog. All of them, of course, display your Unconditional Love for the dog. But they also serve a number of other, equally important functions:

The Six-Pointed Mogen David Star of Pampering

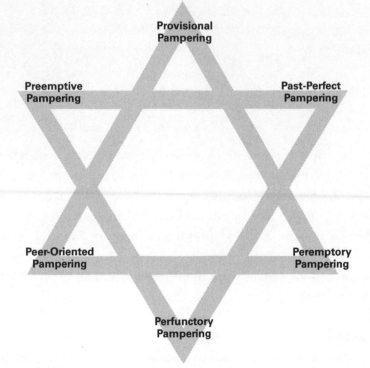

Provisional
Pampering

Preemptive
Pampering

Past-Perfect
Pampering

Peer-Oriented
Pampering

Peremptory
Pampering

Perfunctory
Pampering

Form of Pampering	Purpose Other Than Showing Unconditional Love	What You Buy for Your Dog
Provisional	To lay groundwork for future guilting	Anything she likes
Preemptive	To make sure dog feels secure about the future	Anything she *may* like next week
Past-Perfect	To make sure dog feels free to change her mind	Anything she *used to* like in the past but doesn't anymore but may start to like again
Peer-Oriented	To make sure dog is secure among her peers	Anything *her friends* like
Peremptory	To make sure you feel secure about dog	Anything *you* like
Perfunctory	To take advantage of miscellaneous opportunities to pamper dog and yourself	Anything on sale

As you can see, with these six different forms of pampering the range of items you can buy for the dog is infinite. If the dog likes it, or used to like it, or her friends like it, or if you like it, it's appropriate. Thus, anything from a squeaky plastic bone to a two-bedroom apartment in Rio de Janeiro can be bought "for the dog."

Still, some products are more important than others. Let's review them now.

Sweaters

Most dogs have coats, and so don't particularly "need" sweaters. Still, when the weather turns cold in autumn and winter, a person or a dog could catch pneumonia and drop dead at any minute, because you never know. So a sweater is always a good idea. Besides, there is no better way to show the world your capacity for love and concern — not to mention style and sophistication — than by strolling around the neighborhood with a dog wearing a sweater.

People have asked us why, since we live in warm, subtropical Florida, we even consider dressing our dogs in sweaters. But, as anyone who lives in or has visited these areas can tell you, whether you're in the humid Deep South or the dry desert Southwest, you spend most of your time in freezing air-conditioning. We ourselves wear sweaters indoors the year-round, and so do our dogs.

Booties

Booties, or small boots, are not particularly appropriate for larger dogs, who will often display their resistance to wearing

Dog in goggles: absolutely necessary when allowing dog to ride in car with head out the window or when shopping at upscale retailers

them by tearing them off with their mouths and eating them. For smaller dogs, however, booties offer protection from snow, ice, slush, and even just cold sidewalks. Booties are also very cute and can form a nice ensemble with sweaters.

Scarves

Unlike sweaters and booties, scarves probably don't keep the dog that much warmer. But they can be very stylish and dashing, so much so that when you see your dog in a scarf you feel good. And if you feel good, then by definition the dog feels good. That's why we recommend that your dog wear scarves — because it makes him happy.

Hats

There is probably no health benefit to be gained by having the dog wear a hat. Still, as long as your dog is going out in a sweater, booties, and scarf, what's the harm?

Toys

One of the best ways to pamper the dog is by giving him toys, and the range of toys available at pet stores or online is immense. Just bear in mind that it is impossible to predict which squeaky bone or nub-covered ball your dog will like (if any), or how long he'll like it before abandoning it forever.

Not only that, but it's also very common for a dog to ignore a pet toy expressly designed for him in favor of one of your shoes, a sock, a stuffed animal, a discarded Barbie doll, an old towel, or any other object in the home.

That's why, when clients ask us which toys they should purchase for their dogs, we generally advise buying one of every toy in the pet store, plus one of everything available online, and letting the dog figure it out. In so doing you'll have satis-

Dog playing with owner's slipper and ignoring high-quality dog toys. Typical.

fied all six categories illustrated in the Six-Pointed Mogen David Star of Pampering *and* you'll have a great story to tell friends and family about how enslaved you are to the (ungrateful) dog.

Case History: Matilda

BY RABBI ALAN

The only time our training method actually ever failed was with Matilda. This dog was the most beautiful Afghan you had ever seen. She was just breathtaking. Talk about "pampering" — people stopped this dog and her owner all the time to marvel at her exquisiteness. We spent a total of six months with Matilda and her owner and were unable to change the dog's behavior in the slightest.

Quite concerned — not to mention puzzled and intrigued — we did something we'd never done before. We called in someone I'll refer to as "Gretchen." Gretchen is a pet psychic. Now, we don't normally employ such people, nor do we typically recommend it for our clients. But we were all at our wits' end. So Gretchen arrived and, in strict one-on-one isolation with the dog, had a session with Matilda.

After an hour Gretchen brought us the bittersweet news that Matilda was impossible to train because *she had absolutely no thoughts*. She had no mental life because she didn't need one. She was *that* beautiful. Matilda got all her physical and emotional requirements just by existing, by being herself. People gave her things and praised her and indulged her and so on, all in the hope that Matilda would acknowledge them with the slightest wag of her elegant tail. In this one rare case all we could do was to help Matilda's owner come to terms with having a thought-free dog by helping her to regard Matilda as a special-needs pet and to readjust her expectations accordingly. That, thank God, worked, and now Matilda and her owner are living happily ever after in Sedona, Arizona.

STANDARD DOG EQUIPMENT

So far we've talked about the "fun stuff." Now let's look at the necessities for owning any kind of dog, and whether or not they're appropriate for raising a Jewish dog.

Collars

Every dog needs a collar, and with the huge selection of materials, colors, and styles available for dogs of every possible size, it is easy to find one that's right for a dog being raised Jewish.

But why stop there? Even the most squat-necked pug is able to wear two or three or more collars at once. Collars are for more than just attaching to leashes and holding licenses and rabies and identification tags. They're jewelry for dogs! Think of them as being like wrist bangles: if two is good, four is better.

In fact, who is to say that you can't find, in a small size, a collar to wear on your wrist that matches your dog's? Not us. We say let's have fun with collars!

Choke Chains

Also called "slip collars," these are metal link collars that you slip through a hole in itself like some kind of magic trick, creating a slipknot that gently strangles the dog when it tries to pull away. While choke chains do superficially resemble silver necklaces, they're too frightening and mechanical for Jewish dogs to wear or for Jewish owners to figure out how to work. Forget them.

Leashes and Lines

Leashes, like collars, can be of leather or nylon. They don't actually *have* to match the collar, but it would be nice. Also, they should reflect the season. No leather in the summer, and certainly no patent leather after Labor Day.

Retractable Leads

A retractable lead is a dog leash on a spring-loaded reel. It plays out or winds back in, depending on where the dog is.

Unlike a conventional leash, therefore, this one can extend out to fifteen feet, at which point the dog can suddenly start running around a tree or a person before the lead can retract. The result is that you get literally all tied up with the person or the tree, plus you have a crazy dog attached and still running around.

In other words, this kind of lead offers the owner raising a Jewish dog many, many opportunities to be victimized by the dog. So it's perfect.

Long retractable leash entangling a stranger. Rabbi Monica pretends she's really sorry.

Muzzles

Muzzles are masks of strapping or leash material formed into a kind of basket shape, to be fitted over the dog's mouth to prevent it from barking or biting.

A dog being raised Jewish should have no need of a muzzle. Such a dog will be too busy wondering whether its owner approves of what it's doing to bite anyone, and too busy consoling its owner for the owner's failure if it starts barking. We can skip this piece of equipment entirely.

Harnesses

A harness fits around the dog's chest, and is often worn instead of a collar for holding the leash and the tags.

Otherwise, the harness is for the husky, who has to drag

sleds across the North Pole, or some other kind of dog that has to perform laborious physical work for a living. Does that sound like a dog being raised Jewish? Of course not.

Bark Collars

These collars work by zapping the dog with a mild electric shock when she barks. They are often used by owners whose neighbors complain about the dog's "excessive" barking.

Please. A dog being raised Jewish does not bark excessively. It might *worry* excessively, but you're not going to give the dog an electric shock for that.

Invisible Fencing

This means of "training" the dog to stay within the boundaries of a certain piece of property consists of an electronic collar, like the bark collar, that is tuned via radio frequencies, or something, to an array of sensors planted around the periphery of the area. Whenever the dog threatens to cross the boundary, he is hit with an electric jolt. With certain breeds, they can be very effective — yes, effective at turning the dog into a prisoner and your home into a prison. Don't even talk to us about these.

Tags

Collars are used to hold the dog license and rabies inoculations tags, as well as tags showing general information about the dog's name and home address. Such a dog tag, no matter how complete its information, is barely sufficient, the world being what it is. When it comes to raising a Jewish dog, remember that it is always better to imagine the worst, and then panic, and then realize you're being silly, and then plan for the worst, than to do nothing or, indeed, anything else.

Therefore your dog should also have an electronic identification chip, which is usually implanted (in an outpatient procedure) under the skin on her shoulder. It can be scanned by a special gun to reveal the dog's name, address, and so forth. Think about having two of them implanted, in case one malfunctions. And three, of course, is even better.

It's also a good idea to equip the dog with another collar, of the LoJack variety, which emits a constant radio beacon, in case the dog is kidnapped or runs away. Note that *both of these possibilities are extremely unlikely* for a dog being raised Jewish. The dog will feel guilty if it even thinks about running away, and it will barely be out of your sight long enough to be kidnapped. But why take chances?

Signs

When you first acquire the dog, use either your home computer or one at a local copy center to create an attractive flyer with the dog's photograph, name, and address, with the caption "NOT MISSING *YET*." Distribute these to every home and store in a two-mile radius and post them on as many utility poles and trees as you can. Then you'll be ready if the unthinkable happens. Just because it's unthinkable doesn't mean it's unhappenable.

Bowls

Every dog needs two bowls: one for food and one for water.

Of course, when you talk about raising a Jewish dog, the question naturally arises: Should the dog keep kosher? Such a dog would need three bowls: one for dairy-based dishes, one for meat-based dishes, and one for water.

Frankly, we don't believe in keeping kosher, for ourselves or

"Not Missing Yet" sign informs neighbors that dog is not missing. Some trainers call this precaution unnecessary. We say: It couldn't hurt.

our dogs. Observing kashrut (the kosher dietary laws) is almost always a tenet of Orthodox Judaism, to which neither we nor our dogs subscribe.

On the other hand, Rabbi Monica has told us of a practice her mother used to observe, which we have come to refer to around the Seminary as "Reform kashrut." It involves using two sets of dishes and plates: One for normal, everyday use and one for Chinese takeout, with all its pork and shrimp dishes. You can do this if you wish, but it, too, is not necessary.

A Jewish dog's food bowl should be as big as possible, for reasons we discussed in chapter 5. But it wouldn't kill you to have two food bowls.

Beds

Commercial dog beds are in effect giant round pillows, usually covered with a removable, washable, decorative cover with a soft top surface. Do you need one, when raising a Jewish dog?

Yes. But not for the reason you might expect.

Remember that the dog should sleep with you, in your bed. But, depending on many factors (how large the dog, how many dogs you have, how large your bed, whether you share your bed with another person), there may be times when sleeping space is at a premium. After ordering the dog to move over, or move down to the foot of the bed, you may find you still need more room and order the dog to sleep on the dog bed.

What if she doesn't obey?

In that case, say "All right, fine. You stay here. *I'll* sleep on your bed." Then get out of your bed and curl up on the dog bed until the dog, duly guilted, joins you. Then get back into your bed.

"Guilting" the dog by pretending to agree to sleep in his bed. Because some dogs don't respond well to guilting, you should always buy a dog bed that's comfortable enough for you to sleep on.

ANCILLARY EQUIPMENT

Once you have obtained all the standard items, and have pampered the dog in all six ways, you may discover that your current living situation makes it difficult or impossible to manage all the gear and equipment you have acquired. What good does it do the dog if you can't transport, store, and organize all his, and your, stuff?

That's why we see nothing wrong with moving from your current dwelling into a larger house or apartment, or getting a second house or apartment, or a larger car, or a truck, for this purpose. As we note regarding Peremptory Pampering, you are entitled to get anything *you* like in the service of pampering the dog.

A new home and/or car will not only make it easier to pamper the dog, but will improve your own life — one more reason why dogs are wonderful.

Chapter 7

The Jewish Dog's Physical, Psychological, Mental, and Emotional Health

"**A**s long as you have your health, you have everything. And as long as your dog has his or her health, he or she has everything."

We've all heard this truism — which refers to *physical* health — over the years, and, at least with regard to ordinary dogs, it is as true today as it ever was.

However, things are more complicated when you're raising a Jewish dog. This is not to say that a Jewish dog's physical health isn't important; it's extremely important, and the owner should approach it with a combination of concerned attention and intelligent oversight, enhanced with mild anxiety, plunging fear, and unrestrained hysteria.

But, increasingly, science has shown that a Jewish dog's mental and emotional health is in many ways even more important. We're not surprised. After all, the central fact of the Jewish dog's life is psychological — that is, his relationship with the owner.

That's why we've taken to saying around the Seminary, "As

Importance of Mental Health in Common Household Pets

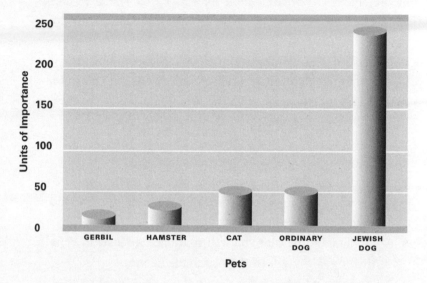

long as you, and the dog, have your psychological, mental, and emotional health, you have everything. Because if you don't, you can't get out of bed. And then who cares about your physical health?"

The graph above illustrates the relative importance of mental and emotional health among Jewish dogs as compared to that of other common household pets.

We'll discuss the dog's mental, emotional, and psychological health (the health that really makes it Jewish) in a moment. First, though, let's address the issue of physical health.

HOW TO GO TO THE VET

Before you can go to a veterinarian, you have to find one. This is easier than it may appear. Simply talk to other dog owners and ask for a referral. Then visit each vet's office, bringing your dog with you. Take special note of the waiting area: if it includes a television tuned to a daytime talk show, leave immediately. A vet whose clientele likes to watch *The Tyra Banks Show* or *The View* will probably fail to appreciate your dog's unique qualities.

Instead, find a waiting room that has magazines that you like, or that you don't mind other people liking. Then ask for a preliminary consultation with the vet. When talking to him or her, look for four qualities:

1. An understanding of how special your dog is
2. An understanding that no one (except the vet) comprehends what you're going through concerning the dog and everything else in your life
3. An understanding that you will spare no expense on behalf of the dog, although you're not made of money
4. An understanding that the dog will (as usual) fail to appreciate all the concern that you and the vet will display toward him, but that you and the vet will just have to live with that, the way you (and, probably, the vet) always do

Once you have selected a vet who is suitably understanding to you and sympathetic about your life, tell him or her that you're "not one of those people who brings the dog in every time there's some tiny problem." Then, from that day forward, bring the dog in every time there's some tiny problem.

When you go in for an appointment and are waiting for the vet, trade pleasant small talk with other owners about how, when the dog is sick, it's like you're sick. If they stare at you blankly and don't understand, ignore them. If they nod and agree and say that they do understand, ignore them. Because do they? Really?

However, if another owner's response is to be competitive

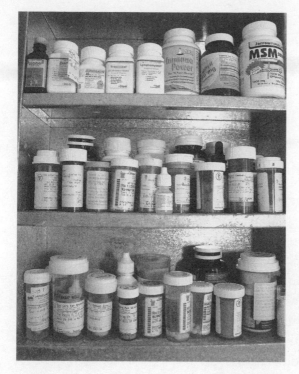

Sample medicine cabinet. Prescriptions not only encompass entire life of current dog, but entire lives of two previous dogs, cat, turtle, and rabbit.

rather than sympathetic (by saying, for example, "You're 'sick'? I would love to be 'sick.' I should be so lucky, 'sick.' When my dog is sick I don't know why I just don't give him a gun and tell him to shoot me"), then that person, too, is raising a Jewish dog, and the two of you will have a lot to talk about. Neither of you will listen to the other, but it will pass the time until the vet is ready to see you. And, if necessary, your dog.

Fill all the vet's prescriptions promptly. Note that, when the dog is cured, there may be some leftover medicine, whose function you don't really understand and which will, sooner or later, expire in potency and be essentially useless. Still, keep it in your own medicine cabinet for the rest of your life, "just in case." And don't be afraid to spend a fortune on homeopathic drugs, vitamins, supplements, and so forth, that don't require a prescription and allow you to medicate, or pretend-medicate, the dog on your own.

Case History: Maddie

BY RABBI MONICA

Jacqueline had just adopted Maddie, a fifty-pound sheltie-collie mix. After about the first month, at about two in the morning, Jacqueline was awakened by a horrible groaning sound. She flew out of bed to find Maddie on the cold tile floor at the bottom of the stairs. She tried to rouse the dog, but Maddie just looked at her and didn't move. Jacqueline carried her to the car and raced to the ER. However, by the time she got there, Maddie was her old self. Naturally, Jacqueline insisted that the vets run all the tests anyway, but every test came back normal. Jacqueline was distraught.

About ten days later, Jacqueline was reading in bed with Maddie beside her. Suddenly Maddie made the horrible groaning sound again. It was then that Jacqueline realized that this noise was Maddie's "sound of contentment." As with a bark, each dog's sound of contentment and happiness is distinctive and unique. In Maddie's case, as in the case of many Jewish dogs, the sound of contentment was practically indistinguishable from the sound of the dog in pain.

YOUR DOG'S MENTAL HEALTH

One of the characteristic behaviors of a Jewish dog is to become withdrawn or irritable from time to time. If you see your own dog acting this way, rest assured that it is normal. Do not do what you customarily do when he gets a physical injury, that is, do not become hysterical and rush him to the vet. Such a response, no matter how well it has served you (and possibly the dog) in the past, is inappropriate for this kind of problem.

This problem is psychological, not physical. It occurs when the owner loves the dog so very, very much, and wants only what's best for the dog, and tells the dog what to do and how to behave only for the dog's own good, and ignores the dog's protests because the owner is a person and the dog is just a dog, that it all becomes a little too much. The dog recoils. He feels as if his "self" isn't being appreciated, or is being smothered, or obliterated, or whatever. He gets angry. But he can't lash out and express his anger at the owner because he'll get into trouble and be punished. And so he swallows his anger.

He becomes depressed.

Now, in previous generations, an owner faced with such behavior from the dog would simply throw up her hands, or tell the dog to go to his room until he cheered up or snapped out of it, or complain to others that the dog is moody. But today's owners are different. They're more enlightened and more informed about human, and dog, nature.

Today's owner understands that the dog has a point.

She realizes that she has been oppressing the dog in exactly the ways in which *she* was oppressed when she was a child. (You will recognize this as relating to stage 4, "Comfort and Reconciliation," of the Basic "Training" Procedure in chapter 3.) She feels terrible. She should know better! In fact she does know better. But now what should she do to help the dog?

Bear in mind that these gloomy feelings, and the depressive lying around and staring and sighing and moping that they lead to, form a "negative loop" in which the dog becomes trapped. Even if the original event that triggered them is over and done with, still the bad feelings stimulate bad thoughts, which generate more bad feelings.

This can even happen with the relatively minor disappointments of everyday life. A dog who, for example, is sleeping or eating or elsewhere in the home when the mailman arrives, and thus misses his daily opportunity to bark like a maniac and chase the mailman away, may occasionally fall into a "misery spiral" over this relatively unimportant event. Very quickly "I missed the mailman" turns into "I hate my life."

The question then becomes: How do we shut down this negative loop?

We have discovered that in most instances the dog can be "cured" via one or more of a series of positive messages, inspirational sayings, and uplifting bits of life wisdom commonly known as "affirmations."

Now, when humans make use of affirmations, they read and recite them out loud, to the universe, in order to hear themselves say those words. Dogs, of course, can't do this. So we have devised a series of affirmations to be read *to the dog by the owner, about the dog himself.*

The affirmation is read to the dog, who then repeats it to himself until he breaks free of the negative emotional loop and feels better about everything.

We are currently compiling a complete collection of affirmations for dogs, which we intend to publish under the title *Arffirmations*. For now, however, we present a handful of these positive, upbeat messages guaranteed to improve your dog's mood. They appear in the following table, along with the kinds of behavior that can alert you to the problem, and the negative emotional states they are meant to cure.

Dealing with the Depressed Dog: The Affirmations

Dog's Behavior	Negative Emotions	Affirmation to Recite to Dog
Lies listlessly on couch, bed, etc., sighing	Dog thinks all his efforts are futile, that "nothing ever turns out right"	"I am a really great dog and I don't need to be depressed in order to lie on the couch. I can be on the couch without having to be depressed because I am well loved and treasured. And I deserve it."
Acts touchy, irritable	Dog feels trapped in his life, surrounded by mediocrity and tedious routine	"I love my routine. Without routines, there is chaos. I am moody sometimes because that's just the way I change my routine without causing chaos. I am brilliant."
Stares blankly into space, is uncommunicative	Dog harbors unexpressed anger	"I stare blankly into space because I can. I get attention from my owner just by doing nothing. I am great."
Lies with head between paws, doesn't move	Dog feels taken for granted, unappreciated, and a failure	"I have perfected the position where everyone thinks I'm doing nothing, but I am, in fact, ready to pounce at a moment's notice. I am a genius."
Sleeps all the time, refuses to go on walks, eats very little	Dog suffers from anomie, barely has the will to live	"I feel a little bloated so I will pretend I am at a doggy spa. By the morning I will be back to my model figure and feel fabulous, which I already am."
Stares, does nothing all day but watch TV and eat Snausages	Dog is trying to numb self, to escape into distraction and cheap pleasures	"I have been good all week and deserve a reward. I shall watch TV and pop Snausages while sitting on satin pillows. My owner will be thrilled because I have seen her do that, and by emulating her I make her feel good as well. I am extremely thoughtful."

113

Listening to affirmations, dog visualizes actualizing the reality of his vision.

Encourage the dog to recite these affirmations to himself, and before too long he'll feel much better — and so will you.

CHRONIC DEPRESSION: THERAPY VERSUS DRUGS

Occasionally a Jewish dog is subject to chronic depression, which even affirmations cannot alleviate. In such cases, we urge owners to consult with a qualified dog therapist, whether a dog psychologist, a dog whisperer, or a dog acupuncturist. Each offers specific areas of expertise and a range of techniques. For recommendations, ask your vet, other owners, or look online.

(Many clients ask us for referrals to a dog *psychiatrist*. When they do, we decline to offer any recommendations. Quite frankly, we don't believe in psychiatrists for dogs. The notion of a dog being subjected to Freudian analysis is, in our opinion, rather ludicrous. We don't see the usefulness of having the dog jump up on a couch and lie there for fifty minutes, when jumping on the couch is often one of the very problems the owner wants to address!)

Sometimes a therapist will diagnose a chemical imbalance in the dog that has triggered this depression. In such cases, one of several canine antidepressants may be prescribed. The most popular and trustworthy ones include:

- Rexapro™: Primarily prescribed for dogs named Rex, this drug has lately also been proven effective with dogs named Rocky.

- Spanielavil™: Prescribed mainly for sporting dogs, Spanielavil has side effects that include excessive friskiness, drooling, and uncontrollable ear floppiness.

- Boxil™: Originally developed for boxers, this drug has a user base that has expanded to include pugs, bulldogs, Boston terriers, and other breeds with mashed-in faces.

- Schnauzoloft™: Proven unusually effective with mixed breeds, or mutts, although during initial stages of use special care should be taken to avoid accompanying owners driving or operating heavy machinery.

- Welshbutrin™: Especially valued for its minimal sexual side effects, although many owners report an increased tendency for their dogs to chase their own tails.

Other medications are available. Owners should be sure to consult a qualified canine psychopharmacologist for a proper diagnosis and prescription, and not just order blindly from the many dog drug Web sites that, unfortunately, have begun to proliferate online.

EMOTIONS, BEHAVIOR, AND YOU

No book written for the general public can possibly deal with all potential physical and emotional problems of every kind of dog. Each breed has its own weaknesses and susceptibilities, and each dog-owner relationship has its own specific characteristics.

Therefore, the Q&A below is intended to discuss some general problem-solving approaches. All dogs referred to have been, or currently are, raised Jewish.

Q: My dog is normally well behaved, but when my decorator Harriet comes to the house, she wears a bit more makeup than we're used to, and it scares the dog and he barks at her. What do I do?

A: This is not the dog's fault. Too much makeup can indeed be frightening. Either start to wear a lot of makeup yourself, to accustom the dog to it, or tell Harriet to wear a mask.

Q: Every day my dog, Peaches, barks at the mailman, both when he comes to our house and ten minutes later, when he crosses from house to house on the other side of the street. Why is this, and can it be remedied?

A: Peaches may be reacting to a dim ancestral memory from her Jewish forebears who lived in New York, Chicago, Baltimore, and other cities in the nineteen teens and twenties. She may believe that the mailman, with his distinctive cap, is a streetcar conductor coming to ask you for money that, she somehow knows, you need not pay. So she chases the "conductor" away until the next day. To remedy this situation, try inviting the mailman in for a cup of coffee or, preferably, for an overnight stay. After a few visits the dog will regard the mailman as neither an intruder nor a streetcar conductor, but as a member of the family. If this solution proves to be impractical, get a post office box.

Q: I am raising my dog, Cassie, to be a Reform Jew. Now she insists on sitting on my lap while I'm driving. No matter how often I place her on the passenger seat, she eventually climbs into my lap and sits up, looking out the side window while I have to work the steering wheel around her. What should I do?

A: This is a classic problem. When we first began addressing it in our teaching sessions at the Seminary, we advised hiring a chauffeur. *Please note that we do not recommend this solution any longer.* Experience has taught us that the dog usually just sits in the chauffeur's lap. Our current thinking on this matter leads us to suggest that you teach her to drive. Naturally, you will have to work the pedals. But there is no reason she can't learn to turn the steering wheel, so long as you keep your hands on it as a precaution.

Q: My dog doesn't like my new boyfriend. What should I do? And by the way, both my boyfriend and I are Jewish. So that's not the issue.

A: Is your boyfriend a mailman or a decorator who wears makeup? If so, see above. If not, talk to your boyfriend and find out what he's doing wrong. Is he teasing or tormenting the dog? Does he own a cat or other animal whose scent your dog might find objectionable? These and similar complaints can be dealt with specifically. Otherwise, dump him.

Q: My Rhodesian ridgeback just sits, completely motionless, and stares at his bowl of dog biscuits. He does this for ten or fifteen minutes at a time. Why? Is this healthy? Is he insane or what?

A: One theory concerning this kind of behavior holds that earlier generations of dogs were able, through the sheer force of their mental emanations, to teleport small objects (sticks, bones, "cookies") to themselves, but that this ability was bred out over generations. What remains, therefore, is the outer behavior without the inner ability. However, if your dog is Jewish, this hypothesis does not apply. Rather, your dog is simply waiting patiently for you to give him cookies, knowing that you will do so because you just can't help yourself.

Q: We live in a beautiful region of Southern California near some undeveloped areas where wildlife can still be

Rhodesian ridgeback attempting to transport "cookies" to himself via telekinesis. If he sits long enough, owner will arrive and give him cookie, confirming to dog that he actually does possess psychic powers.

found. As a result, possums come and sit on our fence at night, and my dog barks at them nonstop. I drag her inside, but she stands at the door to the backyard and barks anyway. What to do?

A: Purchase, legally and with appropriate registration, a rifle or handgun. Take lessons at a responsible shooting range. Then simply keep killing the possums until they stop coming. If neighbors complain about the noise or the potential danger, explain patiently that you're killing possums because your dog barks at them.

Q: I spent $3,000 on a purebred Afghan and, after three years of my raising her Jewish, all she does is act like a mutt. She lounges around and hangs out with other mutts at the dog park and shows no breeding or class whatsoever. I need this? What's the deal?

A: There is no mystery here. Your dog's friends are all mutts, and she's acting like one of them because your dog just wants to be assimilated and to "fit in." You've raised her as a German Jew as opposed to a Russian Jew. Don't worry about it.

Q: I somehow feel that every aspect of my relationship with my dog is a power struggle. Is this normal?

A: Yes. All relationships are power struggles — or, at least, all relationships between Jewish dogs and their owners, who of course love each other. You would think that any dog with half a brain would be grateful to have such a loving, caring owner. But you know how some dogs are: They think they know everything. Whatever the owner says is automatically wrong. Their friends, who are all dogs and have no experience out in the real world, are always ready to encourage your dog to do whatever the pack is doing, no matter how dangerous or rude or self-destructive or embarrassing. If your dog's friends all said, "Let's jump off a bridge," would your dog jump off a bridge? Yes, he would, thank you. So that's your struggle: to deal with such an ungrateful dog while still loving him in spite of everything. Meanwhile, if you can't live like this, get a cat. At least you know where you stand with cats, who don't even pretend to care about anyone except themselves.

Q: After all I've done for my dog, now he insists on digging up the tulip bulbs. Have you ever heard of such horrible behavior?

A: You wouldn't believe the things we've heard. Still, one benefit of having a dog who digs up the tulip bulbs is, the more you replant the bulbs, the more of a triumph it will be when they grow. You'll then have the double satisfaction of knowing that you raised the dog in spite of everything, and the tulips in spite of the dog — two loving, selfless accomplishments, each full of heartache and sacrifice, stories and complaints, which you'll be able to impress and entertain your friends with forever and ever.

Chapter 8

Traveling with (or without) Your Dog

There are many ways to travel, of course, but we're going to limit our discussion to driving in your own car (as opposed to taking public transportation) and flying. For all other kinds of travel, including hot-air balloons, cruises, and bullet trains, simply apply the following principles.

MAKING YOUR CAR A HOME AWAY FROM HOME OR MAKING YOUR HOME INTO A CAR

Some dogs love riding in cars and some dogs can't stand it. You may have learned which kind your dog is when you first brought her home. Or you may have discovered her car preferences while driving her to and from the vet's office many, many, many, many, many times.

Such short trips can be relatively easy. What about longer car trips, like those taken for vacation, to visit relatives, to attend special events, and so on?

The essential fact to remember when driving with a dog

over an extended period is that *the dog's experience in the car should resemble her normal experience at home as much as possible.*

There are several ways to accomplish this. We'll deal with them in descending order of expense.

1. Transport Entire Home on Flatbed Truck

AVAILABLE TO: Owners whose primary residence is a freestanding house

HOW: Hire home-mover service to lift your entire house off its foundation, place it on a flatbed truck, and drive the house itself to your destination.

PROS: Dog's environment never changes. Home-on-the-road *is* her normal home.

CONS: Elaborate pretrip preparation, including disconnecting plumbing, gas, and electricity. Your home street may not accommodate mover's truck. Roads en route to destination may not accommodate truck with house on flatbed. Prohibitions of riding in house while truck is moving — which means you and dog either must follow in separate car or ride in cab with driver. Driver may not like dog. Dog may not like driver. Driver may not like you. You may not like driver. Truck with house on back must move much more slowly than normal traffic, extending duration of trip. House and truck must wait at destination for your return trip, requiring either driver to be paid to remain on call or a new driver to be hired for return. House must then be positioned, reconnected to plumbing, gas, and electricity.

COST: $$$$

RECOMMENDATION: In a perfect world, we would all do this. Alas, our world is imperfect, and this option is impractical for most owners.

2. *Buy or Rent Mobile Home / Recreational Vehicle (RV)*

AVAILABLE TO: Owners willing to drive large, cumbersome mobile home

PROS: More room than conventional cars, wagons, or SUVs means increased capacity for dog's toys, bowls, master bedroom bed, sofas, and so forth, which can be simply transferred from primary residence.

CONS: Mobile home must be rented, leased, or bought. Need special driver's license to operate. Can be hard getting used to driving and parking large vehicle. Poor mileage means appreciable gasoline costs. Parking at destination may be difficult or impossible.

COST: $$$

RECOMMENDATION: This option, while certainly providing luxury and a bit of "adventure," involves astronomical gas prices and endless parking aggravation. Besides, we're not sure Jews "do" RVs. Forget it.

3. *Acquire Minivan or Sport Utility Vehicle (SUV)*

AVAILABLE TO: Owner able to buy, lease, or rent large vehicle

PROS: More room than conventional cars. Normal driver's license sufficient. Recent models equipped with DVD players for dog's entertainment

CONS: Somewhat expensive. Mileage probably not as good as conventional car's. Capacity for dog's furniture (sofa, bed, and so on) limited

COST: $$

RECOMMENDATION: For short and medium-length trips, a good alternative to flying. What you pay for gas will be less than you save on airfare. Dog feels safe; you feel like big shot, sitting up high in big muscular vehicle.

4. Drive Your Everyday Vehicle

AVAILABLE TO: Any owner with car, van, truck, SUV

PROS: No new vehicle needed. No new license required. No new driving, parking skills required

CONS: Limited room for dog's furniture, toys, home entertainment components, special mats, quilts, et cetera

COST: $

RECOMMENDATION: The most economical and least taxing option. Because who needs all that other aggravation?

Bear in mind that over longer car trips you may choose to stay in a motel overnight. Check in advance to find out which of those along your route allow pets and which do not. Or, to assure your dog's maximum comfort and sense of security, simply park somewhere safe, lock the doors, and sleep with the dog in your car.

TRAVEL BY AIR

As everyone knows, air travel has lately become increasingly complicated and fraught with possible problems (lengthy check-ins, delays, canceled flights). Still, for most destinations, air travel remains the fastest and most efficient mode of conveyance.

Traveling with your dog by air may seem at first like a daunting prospect. But the airlines have vast experience transporting pets. As long as you approach this task methodically and allow sufficient time to do what is required, you should have no trouble.

To start, be aware that some airlines will allow you to bring your dog on board with you only if your dog is of the very smallest size and can be held in your lap or in a small carrier. All other dogs, from medium-sized to large, must be flown as cargo, in the luggage hold of the plane. These pets will need to fly in a carrier or "kennel" that conforms to specific structural

Overfurnished dog carrier. Most airlines will remove everything except the water cup. Still, it's worth a try. Look how much dog likes it!

requirements (although almost all the carriers available at pet stores and large discount chains do). The kennel must be large enough to enable your dog to turn around in it and must be equipped with a water dish.

To assist you, we've created the Jewish Dog's Air Travel Checklist. Photocopy the list, follow its steps, and — to you and your dog — bon voyage!

The Jewish Dog's Air Travel Checklist

☐ Two days before departure, check with airline about its requirements for traveling with dog.

☐ Airline will say dog needs a veterinarian's health certificate not older than thirty days. You don't have one (even though you took dog to vet as recently as the day before) and cannot take the dog in for one in time.

☐ Cancel trip.

☐ Reschedule trip, make appointment with vet, get dog checkup. Ask vet if dog will need tranquilizer for flight. Vet will prescribe and sell you two or three. Ask vet if you can take one of them, too. Vet will laugh and say, "No, they're for dogs." Laugh along but be silently disappointed.

☐ Check your own stock of Valium, Xanax, et cetera. If you're all out, borrow from friends.

☐ Buy dog carrier. Decide which to get by asking yourself, Which would I be most comfortable flying in? Then just give up and buy most expensive.

☐ Twenty-four hours before departure, obsess over how to furnish kennel. Include fluffy towel, dog's favorite toys, T-shirt or sock with your scent. Consider small boom box with dog's favorite music, dish of dog biscuits, laminated photographs of you.

☐ Twelve hours before departure, scan Internet frantically for weather conditions at departure airport, arrival airport, airspace in between. Phone airline and ask if there is any problem with the flight. Airline will say, "It's too soon to know. The flight doesn't leave for twelve hours."

☐ On day of flight, confirm that airline suggests you arrive ninety minutes before departure, but, because you are traveling with dog, you should arrive two hours before departure. Leave home allowing sufficient time to deal with traffic, dog's possible need to pee on side of road, and anything else that could possibly delay your trip.

☐ Arrive at airport five hours before departure. Place dog in kennel by begging, pleading, wrestling, whatever it takes.

☐ Start to wheel luggage and kennel to terminal. Discover that you've accidentally put kennel wheels on wrong, with pivoting wheels in rear and fixed wheels in front. Feel like idiot. Wheel kennel awkwardly entire way, dragging nonpivoting front wheels every time you have to make slightest turn.

☐ At curbside check-in, accept skycap's offer of help. Speak baby talk to dog to reassure her as you get boarding pass. When ticket agent asks questions, get confused. Speak baby talk to agent as you show him driver's license or passport. Hope he doesn't think you're a terrorist.

☐ Follow skycap as he wheels luggage to X-ray machine. Experience sudden nausea as you wonder if security people are going to X-ray dog. Be relieved when they say no.

☐ Follow skycap as he wheels (awkwardly) kennel into terminal. Start to panic as he takes you to unmanned counter and produces walkie-talkie. Be relieved as skycap calls animal control officer to check dog in. Stop panicking and begin feeling anxious. Why animal control officer?

☐ Greet animal control officer, who will inspect kennel. When officer asks, "Where is the water?" resume panicking. Run to airport souvenir shop, pay $3.50 for bottled water, return, spill bottled water on self, dog, skycap, and animal control officer as you pour it into absurdly shallow water dish in kennel.

☐ Be embarrassed when animal control officer asks, "What are these?" Answer, "Oh, just some cookies, a laminated picture of me in case [dog's name] gets anxious, and a small boom box with [dog's name]'s favorite music." Officer will tell you to remove cookies and boom box. Do so, stuffing both into your carry-on bag.

☐ Attempt to give dog tranquilizer. As dog refuses, realize that giving dog pill involves more than just holding it out like a candy. When animal control officer says, "People usually hide the pills in peanut butter," run back to souvenir shop, wait in line, buy soft candy bar or muffin, run back, embed pill in snack, feed to dog. Listen as animal control officer says, "I don't know how long your flight is, but if you're not departing for five hours, I hope that pill lasts."

☐ Debate giving dog second pill. Glare at skycap until he stops laughing. Break second pill in half with thumbnail, shatter pill, watch as it sprays all over self, dog. Be pathetically grateful as animal control officer says, "Don't worry. Your dog will be fine," and wheels dog off (awkwardly).

☐ Feel pang of fear, loss, as you watch dog go.

☐ Wonder why skycap is still standing there. Then realize why. Look in wallet for five-dollar tip. Find only ten-dollar bill. Wonder, for a second, if you should ask him for five dollars change. Decide the hell with it and give him ten.

☐ Go through security. When carry-on is X-rayed, wonder if boom box will make you look like a terrorist. Decide that it does. Wonder why nobody says anything and you're waved on.

☐ Feel immense relief.

☐ Look at clock and say to self, Now what the hell am I going to do for four hours?

☐ Take Valium, Xanax, et cetera.

☐ Walk toward gate. En route, see people in bars drinking beer or cocktails at ten in the morning. Feel repulsed.

☐ Enter bar, get seat, drink beer or cocktails for two hours. Make it three hours.

☐ Finally make it to gate. Use bathroom "one last time."

☐ Board plane, find seat. Immediately start listening for sound of dog's crying or barking coming from underneath cabin. Hear nothing.

☐ Relax. Pass out.

☐ Half an hour into flight, suddenly jerk awake. Listen for dog, hear nothing. Decline headphones for movie so you can spend entire flight listening for dog, hearing nothing, and "reading" while looking up at in-flight entertainment every five minutes. Watch but do not hear Adam Sandler in stupid movie for an hour and a half.

☐ Land. Go crazy waiting for people in front to file out of plane. Ask silently, How hard can it be to get your damn bag and walk down the aisle?

☐ Go to baggage claim. Ask uniformed person where to meet dog. Nod and apologize as uniformed person says, "Sorry, ma'am, I don't know. I'm in the marines."

☐ Find cargo delivery window. Rejoice as kennel is brought out with dog awake, perky, happy to see you. Remove dog from kennel and peer, smell inside, fearing worst. Be relieved dog didn't pee in kennel. Put leash on dog and walk outside terminal, looking for and not finding grassy area. Allow dog to pee wherever she wants.

☐ Return to terminal, place dog back in kennel "just for now," and wait for luggage. Or, if being met by someone, turn dog on leash over to him.

☐ Assemble luggage, wheel bags and kennel (awkwardly) out terminal to car or cab.

☐ Realize that you will have to do all this all over again for return trip.

PET SITTERS

Sometimes, as on vacations or business trips, we find ourselves having to travel without our pets. Who will feed, walk, play with, despair of, and apologize to the dog in our absence?

If you don't have someone else in your household (such as a spouse or roommate), and don't want to ask your neighbors, and dislike the physical confinement and exposure to other dogs that comes with a kennel stay, consider finding a dog sitter.

Such a person usually moves into your home for the express purpose of living with and caring for your dog. That's why, even for just minding an ordinary dog, a sitter must be selected with great care. When it comes to minding a Jewish dog, with his more elaborate emotional and psychological ties to his caregiver, a sitter must be uncompromisingly trustworthy and come with impeccable credentials.

For this reason we've developed the Boca Raton Theological Seminary Comprehensive Multiphasic Biographical and Personality Dog Sitter Intake Workup Profile Questionnaire. Feel free to photocopy it for each candidate you interview when searching for a dog sitter. Instructions on how to "score" the B.R.T.S.C.M.B.P.D.S.I.W.P.Q. appear following the form itself.

THE BOCA RATON THEOLOGICAL SEMINARY COMPREHENSIVE MULTIPHASIC BIOGRAPHICAL AND PERSONALITY DOG SITTER INTAKE WORKUP PROFILE QUESTIONNAIRE

NAME _____

ADDRESS _____

PHONE NUMBER (DAY) _____

PHONE NUMBER (EVE) _____

PHONE NUMBER (MOBILE) _____

OCCUPATION _____

DISTANCE FROM HOME TO WORK _____

HOURS _____

HOW LONG HAVE YOU BEEN EMPLOYED
AT THIS JOB? _____

YEARLY SALARY _____

OTHER INCOME _____

SAVINGS _____

OWN OR RENT? _____

MARRIED _____ SINGLE _____ DIVORCED _____

HOW MANY YEARS? _____

HOW MANY CHILDREN? _____

AGES _____

PARENTS ALIVE OR DEAD? _____

ADDRESS _____

RETIRED? _____

HAVE YOU EVER BEEN ARRESTED? _____

WHAT FOR? _____
_____
_____

HAVE YOU EVER BEEN CONVICTED OF A CRIME APART
FROM MINOR TRAFFIC OFFENSES? _____

WHICH ONE(S)?_____
_____
_____
_____

MEDICAL HISTORY

INTERESTING MEDICAL STORIES_____
_____
_____
_____
_____
_____
_____

CURRENT MEDICATIONS _____
_____
_____
_____
_____
_____
_____

PAST MEDICATIONS _____
_____
_____
_____
_____
_____
_____

ARE YOU ALLERGIC TO ANYTHING? _____

ARE YOU ALLERGIC TO DOGS? _____

IF "YES," WHY DO YOU WANT TO "DOG-SIT"?_____
_____
_____

HAVE YOU EVER TAKEN OR USED AN
ILLEGAL SUBSTANCE? _____

WHICH ONE(S)? _____
_____
_____

DO YOU DRINK ALCOHOLIC BEVERAGES?_____

WHICH ONE(S)? _____
_____
_____

HOW OFTEN? _____

WHAT KINDS? THE GOOD STUFF _____
HOUSE BRAND _____
WHATEVER'S AVAILABLE _____

ARE YOU NOW OR HAVE YOU EVER BEEN IN THERAPY? _____

IF YES, FOR WHAT?_____
_____
_____

NAME OF THERAPIST _____

HOURLY RATE (AT THE TIME OF YOUR TREATMENT) _____

PHONE NUMBER _____

WILL YOU WAIVE DOCTOR/PATIENT
CONFIDENTIALITY AND ALLOW ME TO REVIEW YOUR
THERAPIST'S EVALUATION?_____

IF NO, WHY NOT? DO YOU HAVE SOMETHING TO HIDE? _____

IF YES, WHAT? _____
_____
_____
_____

ARE YOU CURRENTLY ON ANTIDEPRESSANTS? _____

WHICH ONE(S)? _____
_____
_____
_____

HAVE YOU EVER BEEN ADDICTED TO ANY SUBSTANCE? _____

TO ANY BEHAVIOR? (E.G., GAMBLING, SEX) _____

ANY WEIRD PHOBIAS? _____

IF YES, WHICH ONE(S)? _____

YOU'RE KIDDING. SERIOUSLY? _____

SPIRITUAL PROFILE

ARE YOU RELIGIOUS? _____

IF YES, WHICH DENOMINATION?
CHRISTIAN _____ JEWISH _____ MUSLIM _____
BUDDHIST _____ HINDU _____
GENERAL NEW AGE /"WOO-WOO" _____

CHURCH/SYNAGOGUE/MOSQUE AFFILIATION? _____ _____

ADDRESS _____
_____

DO YOU TALK TO GOD? _____

DOES GOD TALK BACK TO YOU? _____

DO YOU BELIEVE IN AN AFTERLIFE? _____

DO YOU THINK THE DOG'S OWNER WILL GO TO HELL FOR
LEAVING THE DOG WITH A STRANGER? _____

PERSONAL BACKGROUND

DID YOU GROW UP WITH A DOG? _____

WAS THE DOG A MEMBER OF THE FAMILY OR A PET? _____

WHERE OR FROM WHOM DID YOU GET THE DOG? _____

WHO WAS RESPONSIBLE FOR THE DOG? _____

WHY DO YOU WANT TO DOG-SIT NOW? _____
_____
_____

DID YOU HAVE A DOG BEFORE
(AFTER LEAVING HOME)? _____

WHAT HAPPENED TO THE DOG? _____
_____
_____

IF THE DOG DIED, WHAT DID THE DOG DIE OF? _____
_____
_____
_____

PREVIOUS VET'S NAME AND NUMBER _____
_____

SPECIALIST'S NAME AND NUMBER _____

DO YOU OWN A DOG NOW? _____

NAME _____

AGE _____

WHAT BREED? _____

NICE? _____

WILL SOMEONE ELSE DOG-SIT YOUR DOG
WHILE YOU'RE DOG-SITTING MINE? _____

IF YES, DOES YOUR DOG SITTER HAVE A DOG? _____

WHO WILL DOG-SIT YOUR DOG SITTER'S DOG WHILE
YOUR DOG SITTER IS DOG-SITTING YOUR DOG WHILE YOU
ARE DOG-SITTING MINE? _____
_____

(REPEAT THIS QUESTION UNTIL ARRIVING AT A DOG SITTER WHO
DOES NOT OWN A DOG HIM/HERSELF.)

WHAT IS THE NAME OF THE DOG SITTER WHO
DOES NOT OWN A DOG? _____

PHONE NUMBER _____

CELL NUMBER _____

IF YOU AREN'T MARRIED, ARE YOU
DATING ANYONE NOW? _____

LIVING WITH? _____

PLAN TO GET MARRIED? _____

BIG WEDDING? _____

DO YOU WANT CHILDREN? _____

WHEN DID YOU LOSE YOUR VIRGINITY? _____

WHAT IS YOUR FAVORITE MOVIE? _____

WHAT KIND OF MUSIC DO YOU LIKE? _____

WHAT KIND OF MUSIC DO YOU
ABSOLUTELY HATE? _____

WHAT IS YOUR FAVORITE BOOK? _____

WHAT IS YOUR FAVORITE TV SHOW? _____

DO YOU HAVE TIVO? _____

DO YOU WATCH HGTV? OR ESPN? _____

WHAT'S YOUR FAVORITE
TYPE OF FOOD? _____

ARE YOU MAC OR PC? _____

WHAT KIND OF CAR DO YOU DRIVE? _____

OWN OR LEASE? _____

ARE YOU AN INTROVERT OR AN EXTROVERT? _____

DO YOU LIKE TO GO TO PARTIES OR THROW THEM? _____

DO YOU READ *PEOPLE* OR *THE NEW YORKER*? _____

DO YOU DO CROSSWORD PUZZLES? _____

IN PEN OR PENCIL? _____

REGULAR OR CRYPTIC? _____

WHAT IS YOUR GREATEST REGRET? _____
_____

WHAT COLLEGE DID YOU GO TO? _____

DID YOU GRADUATE? _____

YEAR _____

MAJOR _____

WHO'S YOUR OLDEST FRIEND? _____

WHO'S YOUR NEWEST FRIEND? _____

DO YOU HAVE A LOT OF FRIENDS OR A SMALL,
TIGHT-KNIT CIRCLE? _____

DO YOU HAVE SIBLINGS? _____

ARE YOU CLOSE? _____

DO THEY HAVE DOGS? _____

DO THEY HAVE KIDS WHO COME TO VISIT YOU? _____

DO YOU BELIEVE O.J. WAS GUILTY? _____

ARE YOU A DEMOCRAT OR A REPUBLICAN? _____

DO YOU VOTE? _____

DO YOU KNOW WHO THE PRESIDENT OF
THE UNITED STATES IS? (Y/N) _____

WHO IS HE/SHE? _____

DO YOU KNOW WHO THE VICE PRESIDENT IS? (Y/N) _____

WHO IS HE/SHE? _____

DO YOU KNOW HOW MUCH YOUR
STATE'S SALES TAX IS? _____

HOW MUCH? _____

HOW MANY SUPREME COURT JUDGES ARE THERE? _____

HOW MANY TIME ZONES ARE THERE
IN THE UNITED STATES? _____

DO YOU BELIEVE IN UFOS? _____

WHO IS STEVEN SPIELBERG MARRIED TO? _____

DO YOU KNOW WHO EDDIE IZZARD IS? _____

DO YOU PREFER FLORALS OR PLAIDS? _____

IF THERE WAS AN ACCIDENT AND BOTH YOUR DOG AND YOUR
CHILD GOT HURT, WHO WOULD YOU TAKE TO THE DOCTOR FIRST?
_____

WHAT IS YOUR DAY-TO-DAY LIFE LIKE? _____
_____
_____
_____

WHAT DO YOU IMAGINE YOUR DAY-TO-DAY LIFE WILL
BE LIKE WHILE DOG-SITTING? _____
_____
_____
_____
_____
_____
_____
_____
_____
_____
_____
_____

WHAT SACRIFICES DO YOU ANTICIPATE HAVING TO MAKE
IN ORDER TO BE A GOOD DOG SITTER? _____
_____
_____
_____
_____
_____
_____
_____
_____
_____
_____
_____
_____
_____

WILL THE DOG GET TO RIDE IN THE FRONT SEAT
WITH THE WINDOW DOWN? _____

DO YOU BELIEVE DOGS SHOULD SLEEP IN THE
SAME BED WITH THEIR OWNERS? _____

SHOULD YOU ALLOW YOURSELF TO BE
SEEN NAKED BY YOUR DOG? _____

WHAT'S YOUR FAVORITE COLOR COMBINATION? _____

NAME THE LAST THREE PEOPLE YOU HAD A
ROMANTIC RELATIONSHIP WITH. _____
_____
_____
_____
_____

WHY (IN YOUR OPINION) DIDN'T IT WORK OUT? _____
_____
_____
_____
_____

ARE YOU STILL "FRIENDS" WITH THEM? _____

DO YOU EXERCISE REGULARLY? _____

DO YOU BUY THINGS OFF EBAY? _____

DO YOU SELL THINGS ON EBAY? _____

DO YOU PREFER PILATES OR YOGA? _____

HOW OFTEN DO YOU GET YOUR HAIR CUT? _____

DO YOU LIKE TO TRY DIFFERENT STYLES?_____

DO YOU TRY DIFFERENT HAIR COLORS? _____

DO YOU LIKE TO LISTEN TO MUSIC? _____

WHAT KIND? _____

HAS LIFE DISAPPOINTED YOU? _____

WHAT WAS THE LONGEST TIME YOU EVER WAITED
ON LINE FOR SOMETHING? _____

WHAT WAS IT FOR? _____

IF YOU'RE DRIVING AND TRAFFIC COMES TO A STANDSTILL,
DO YOU GET OFF THE HIGHWAY AND TRY AND FIND ANOTHER
ROUTE OR DO YOU WAIT FOR TRAFFIC TO START MOVING AGAIN?
_____
_____
_____

WOULD YOU LIE IN ORDER NOT TO HURT SOMEONE'S FEELINGS?
_____

ARE YOU A HEAVY OR LIGHT SLEEPER? _____

DO YOU MAKE/KEEP NEW YEAR'S RESOLUTIONS? _____

IF THERE WAS ONE THING ABOUT YOURSELF YOU COULD
CHANGE, WHAT WOULD IT BE? _____

DO YOU PREFER POTTERY BARN OR
CRATE AND BARREL? _____

WHAT TYPE OF SNEAKERS DO YOU WEAR? _____

HOW OFTEN DO YOU BUY NEW ONES? _____

ARE YOU BRAND-LOYAL OR DO YOU BUY
WHATEVER'S ON SALE? _____

HAVE YOU EVER SENT A BOTTLE OF WINE
BACK AFTER TASTING IT? _____

DO YOU PREFER WATCHING FOOTBALL ON TV
OR GOING TO THE GAME? _____

WHAT WAS YOUR FAVORITE SANDWICH AS A KID?_____
_____

WHAT WAS THE FIRST CONCERT YOU WENT TO?_____
_____

WHAT DO YOU WISH YOU HAD MORE TIME FOR? _____
_____

COMPLETE: CATS ARE STUPID BECAUSE _____
_____
_____
_____

THE B.R.T.S.C.M.B.P.D.S.I.W.P.Q.: HOW TO EVALUATE

There are no quantitative dimensions to the B.R.T.S.C.M.B.
P.D.S.I.W.P.Q. Rather than try to score it, therefore, just read
over the candidate's answers. By the time you get to the end,
you'll know if this is someone you want to trust with your dog,
and your home, in your absence.

Chapter 9

Getting Older

For dogs as well as for humans, the process of aging seems to involve a series of trade-offs: We lose acuity in vision and hearing but gain a more stable emotional equilibrium. We lose a certain amount of physical robustness but gain insight into ourselves and others. Our memory isn't what it used to be, and yet at the same time our memory isn't what it used to be.

This is especially true for the owner and the dog he or she has been raising for a longer period of time. You both may suffer a certain loss of physical vitality, but the relationship between you will have strengthened, matured, and grown. Lessons the dog once had to be taught (or reminded of) with painstaking patience have long since been learned. Commands that formerly required lengthy rhetorical or sarcastic questions now need only a word or two.

In fact, every aspect of the owner-dog relationship that we've discussed in the preceding chapters will, by seven or eight years into the relationship, have changed in subtle but noticeable ways. We'll review them now so you'll know what to anticipate in the future.

THE INNER MONOLOGUES: LESS IS MORE

The inevitable changes that accompany aging can be seen in a comparison of two of the Inner Monologues belonging to "Jeff," an owner raising a Jewish dog. The first was recorded when he was thirty-three years old and had just acquired Flash, a one-year-old wheaten terrier. The second was recorded after sharing a relationship with the dog lasting a dozen years.

EVOLUTION OF INNER MONOLOGUES: "JEFF" (OWNER, MALE)

Phase I: Age 33

WHOA! — THIS DOG IS NUTS! WHAT — HEY! HE'S PEEING ON THE FL—! OH, WELL. HE'S A PUPPY. HOW DO I GET HIM TO SIT STILL SO I CAN PUT THE LEASH ON. DOES HE KNOW WHAT "SIT" MEANS?... OBVIOUSLY NOT. OKAY, FINE, JUMP AROUND LIKE A MANIAC. GOOD THING DEBBIE LIKES YOU, PAL. YEAH, OKAY, KISSES, KISSES... GOTCHA! OKAY, OUTSIDE! OW! PULLING MY ARM OFF...

Phase II: Age 45

OH, GREAT. THE MAIL... GODDAMN IT. WHAT THE HELL AM I PAYING A THOUSAND DOLLARS A MONTH FOR HEALTH INSURANCE IF IT DOESN'T COVER ANYTHING? OKAY, FINE. JUST — ALL RIGHT, LOOK, WHERE'S DEBBIE? HOW COME I'M ALWAYS THE ONE WHO HAS TO WALK THE DOG? AND WHERE ARE THE KIDS? THIS IS THEIR JOB, GODDAMN IT. OW! GODDAMN IT... NOW WHAT? ARE WE GOING OUTSIDE OR WHAT? JESUS, DON'T DO ME ANY FAVORS...

Of course, it's not just the owner who benefits from the maturing of the relationship over the years. Here are the Inner Monologues of Flash.

EVOLUTION OF INNER MONOLOGUES: FLASH (WHEATEN TERRIER, MALE)

Phase I: Age 1

FUN! YAY! JUMP JUMP JUMP! WHAZZAT!? IT'S THE LEASH! YAY! JUMP JUMP JUMP! WHAT? "SIT"? WHAZZAT? FUN! SPIN SPIN SPIN SPIN SPIN SPIN! YAY! OUTSIDE! OUTSIDE! YA-A-A-A-A-YYY YAY! JUMP . . . JUMP . . . "SIT"? YAY! SIT SIT SIT SIT SIT SIT SIT SIT SIT! OUTSIDE! FUN! OW! OH, "SIT"! OKAY. LEASH. HERE WE GO!

Phase II: Age 13

WHAT? OUTSIDE? WHATEVER. LEASH? FINE. LIKE I'M RUNNING AWAY SOMEWHERE. SIT? THAT I CAN DO. BELIEVE ME, SITTING IS NO PROBLEM. THERE. SURE, LET'S GO. YOU'RE THE BOSS. OY. I NEED A REST.

This parallel evolution of the Inner Monologues of both owner and dog is characteristic of our Program for raising a Jewish dog. You age, the dog ages, and the relationship ages. Eventually nobody remembers who is who.

THE PICS SYSTEM OF MEMORY ENHANCEMENT

It's a sad truth about getting older that we — and when we say "we" we always mean, we humans *and* our dogs — become less able to remember things. We lose the ability to remember names, events, the location of objects we held in our hands not two minutes ago, the spelling of certain words, the authors of books, the titles of books, and whether we've actually read the books.

The dog, too, is subject to this deterioration of memory. An older dog will, for example, gaze blankly at a bedroom slipper, rag doll, or other formerly beloved object, as though trying to remember why it looks familiar.

To assist both owner and dog with this problem, we have developed what we call the Pictorial/Informational Cueing System, or PICS. We began with the informal folk remedy of posting sticky notes on mirrors, computer screens, refrigerator doors, and so on, to remind people of phone numbers, errands, and the like. Then we thought, Well, why not go "all the way" and develop a system of posting the names of appliances, furniture, et cetera, to help people remember what they are?

But then we ran into a problem. Yes, labels around the house would help the owner remember what was what — but how to help the dog? Dogs, for all their miraculous abilities, can't read, after all.

But they can see, and they recognize items by sight. So PICS calls for the owner to take snapshots of the most important items in the dog's daily line of vision and affix them to those items as a way of reminding the dog what they are.

The accompanying photograph shows how simple — but also how helpful — PICS can be for both dog and owner.

BASIC TRAINING IN THE LATER YEARS

In chapter 3 we introduced you to our Basic "Training" Procedure. It consisted of a Five-Stage Cycle that included the following steps:

*Elderly dog, afflicted with failing eyesight, uses PICS system of object identification.
Looking at photograph of window on window, he confirms that window is window.*

1. **Unconditional Love:** You pampered and adored the dog
   without limit or preconditions.
2. **The Great Betrayal:** When you issued a command to the
   dog, and she failed to obey, you reacted as though she were
   deliberately defying you and displaying ingratitude for all
   you had done for her.
3. **Conditional Unconditional Love:** You "guilted" the dog,
   openly wondering why you bothered to show her all this
   love if "this" was how she was going to repay you. You col-
   lapsed, sobbing, openly moaned to strangers.
4. **Comfort and Reconciliation:** The dog, thus guilted, dis-
   played concern for you. Duly comforted, you realized that
   you knew better than to act like this, that your feeling victimized was crazy, and so on. You apologized to the dog
   and to any remaining bystanders.

5. Enlightened Acceptance: You withdrew the original command and, with the dog, you worked together to solve the problem.

This cycle will be relevant in training situations for most of the dog's life. But by the time the dog is eight or nine (for large dogs) or eleven or twelve (for medium-sized and smaller dogs), the Basic "Training" Procedure will have become moot, and another procedure will take its place.

This diagram outlines the next five-step cycle.

The Elderly Dog/Owner "Training" Procedure:
The Five-Stage Cycle

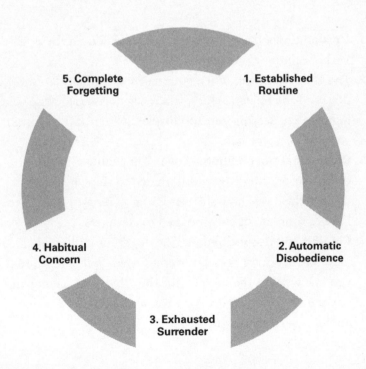

The Elderly Dog/Owner "Training" Procedure: What the Terms Mean

1. **Established Routine:** You and the dog go about your daily routine: walking, feeding, cuddling, talking. As part of this routine, you give some command to the dog.

2. **Automatic Disobedience:** The dog fails to obey the command because she always has (and always will). It's part of the routine.

3. **Exhausted Surrender:** You perceive that the dog has been disobedient. Rather than feel betrayed (as you used to), by now you just don't care. You're "too tired to deal with this." Or you're "too old for this kind of thing." In any case, you "give up." You say, out loud, "Look, never mind. I give up."

Rabbi Alan, having just issued command for ten thousandth time, and elderly dog, having again disobeyed it, reach final stage of cycle and no longer remember what they were talking about, what the issue was, or who the other is.

4. **Habitual Concern:** The dog, after years of exposure to your giving up, knows that you are unhappy. By sheer force of habit, she comes to you, or at least looks over at you. It might mean she is apologizing for being disobedient. It might mean she is waiting for you to give the command again. Or it might mean that the dog is trying to remember who you are. Any of these establishes the conditions for the final stage.

5. **Complete Forgetting:** You no longer remember what the command was or why you gave it. And neither does the dog. The entire incident has been completely forgotten and everyone starts over with a clean slate.

This, you will not be surprised to learn, marks the final stage in the "training."

THREE BASIC "COMMANDS" FOR THE OLDER DOG

Just as the Basic "Training" Procedure has to be revised to take into account the characteristics of the older dog (and her owner), so must the Basic Commands.

For most of the dog's life, the commands "Sit!," "Down!," and "Stay!" are the most essential and are used the most frequently.

The older dog, however, requires a different vocabulary of commands.

And we do mean *different*. For one thing, these are not actually "commands." We call them "requests." And, while the Basic Commands are to be delivered in one or more of the Five Modes with increasing emotional intensity and urgency (as explained in chapter 3), the Requests are delivered with one of Three Moods of decreasing emotion.

Controlling the Older Dog: Three Basic Requests in Three Moods				
Basic Request in Mildly Annoyed Mood	What It Calls For	When to Use It	Tired-of Talking-About-It Mood	Acknowledgment-of-Futility Mood
"Don't start."	Tells the dog not to engage in the bad behavior he always engages in	All the time	"Do you hear me?"	"Fine. Do what you want."
"Oh, please."	Tells the dog not to even bother wanting, let alone requesting, the thing at issue, the granting of which is impossible	Whenever necessary	"Out of the question."	"Fine. Whatever."
"I'm talking."	Tells the dog to suppress his desire or intention and let the owner be the focus of whatever is going on	Constantly	"Hello!?"	"Never mind."

The Request is first issued in the Mildly Annoyed Mood; when it is ignored, it is reissued in the Tired-of-Talking-About-It Mood and, when that too doesn't work, in the Acknowledgment-of-Futility Mood, in which the owner gives up.

Practice these Requests in all three of their Moods once your dog reaches his eighth (for large dogs) or eleventh (for smaller dogs) birthday. It may seem tedious to do so at first, but rest assured, you won't have to do it for that long. The older the dog becomes, the less you will need to practice or even use these Requests, because the dog will increasingly ignore them and because you will increasingly just give up ahead of time.

FOUR LITTLE WORDS

Like the prisoners in the old story, who cue each other about their favorite jokes just by shouting out a number, you and the dog will, after many years, become so accustomed to each other's needs, habits, commands, defiance of commands, and everything else that you'll be able to convey them in a series of shorthand references based on a small group of familiar words you will have used literally thousands of times. Of course, unlike the prison jokes, these ideas can't be presented via numbers. That would be absurd; the dog doesn't know numbers.

He does, however, know the four Useful Words we discussed in chapter 3: "So," "Nu," "What," and "Okay?" After eight or more years of living with the dog, you will have used these terms consistently and repeatedly in a limited and highly meaningful series of contexts. With this in mind, we've been able to devise a fairly comprehensive list of comments, questions, rebukes, and explanations using a "code" based on these four words alone.

The following table shows how to arrange the four words into a number of sentences that a typical owner might use in a common, everyday scenario. Of course, this will be a one-way conversation, since the dog will not be able to reply in actual words. But he'll know what you're saying and be able to respond accordingly.

Longtime Companions: The Four-Word Shorthand Code of Commands and Rebukes

Coded Phrase	Actual Meaning of Phrase
So?	Jesus, what a day. Traffic was a bitch. Ooooh, how's my good boy? How's everything here?
What?	I'm sorry, I can't play with you now. I have to take a shower and finish making dinner. Someone's coming over.
Nu?	Get off the bed, I have to change the sheets. Never mind
Okay?	I don't care if it's raining. You have to pee outside, period.
So nu?	No, don't shake until I dry you with the towel. NO, DON'T. SH——. Goddamn it, now look at the walls.
What, okay?	Here. Eat your dinner. Why are you staring? It's the lamb you like.
So what — Okay? Nu?	I know why. It's because you're waiting for these pork ribs, isn't it?
What so — nu?	Well, forget it. We've discussed this. They splinter and they'll tear up your throat. Besides, it's for company.
Nu, okay? So.	Stop sulking. Here's another cookie, but *no ribs*. Now take it. I have to get the door.
Okay? Nu? What?	Down! Down! Be nice, okay?
So okay? What nu!	What did we say about company? You sniff once and then you find your spot! No humping and no sniffing crotches! I mean it!
Okay? So!	No begging in the dining room. How many times have we talked about this?
What nu, so okay?	He was not supposed to let you have one of those rib bones. Give it back. I'm serious. It is DANGEROUS. Give it back.
What okay? Nu so.	No! Don't you dare growl at him!

Other coded sentences are available on our Web site.

A Final Word from Rabbi Paul

When I founded the Boca Raton Theological Seminary in 1988, I knew two things: one, that I wanted to provide a venue for the training of rabbis within a particularly progressive branch of Judaism that for too long had remained ill served by our nation's established rabbinical colleges and, two, that I was allergic to dogs.

Both are still true today. In fact, they're even truer than they were back then. My commitment to training religious leaders in Reform-Progressive Trans-Diasporatic Neo-Revisionalist Judaism is, if anything, even stronger than when I began. And I'm even more allergic to dogs than ever.

When we began the Seminary there were maybe one or two dogs around, and all I had to worry about was sneezing and itchy, tearing eyes and a runny nose. I tried controlling that with antihistamines, but if you've ever taken one you know what happens: after about two hours they knock you out so that you can't keep your eyes open. One cannot exactly study (let alone teach) Torah and Talmud if one is asleep at one's desk.

From there I moved to the so-called nondrowsy allergy pills (Allegra, Zyrtec, Claritin), and things were more or less under control. But then the dog training program really took off. Instead of one or two dogs here and there on this day or that, suddenly there were six or seven, everywhere, all the time. I began to experience a certain inability to breathe. My lungs felt slightly congested and produced a somewhat comical wheezing sound (not unlike that of a Balkan musical instrument built around a goat's bladder) if, God forbid, I tried to exhale completely.

Now there are ten or more dogs on-site, day in and day out, and it seems I've been blessed with a mild form of allergic asthma. At least that's what the medical technician called it after administering to me the methacholine challenge, where you go to the hospital (in an outpatient procedure) and inhale a series of gases with increasing concentrations of something in them (I don't know what, maybe essence of dog) and then exhale into some kind of

Rabbi Paul, founder of the Boca Raton Theological Seminary, with Allegro

measuring device. With this diagnosis came a prescription for a twice-daily powdered inhalant (Advair) and an emergency inhaler of albuterol, just in case.

A lot of you may now be wondering why I stay when I'm in such physical discomfort. Why, with all my inhalers and allergy pills and boxes of Kleenex and watery eyes, do I remain at this institution?

I used to ask myself the same thing, all the time. I also used to ask, Who needs a bunch of dogs at a religious seminary? How is this whole enterprise appropriate for a place like this?

When I would discuss this dilemma with friends, they would say, "But look at the monks of New Skete! They raise German shepherds and it works out great for them!" And so they do. But they are an order of Catholic celibates living in a cloistered retreat in upstate New York. They run a monastery, where it's traditional to have some secular activity (whether it's bottling brandy or making preserves and jellies or, yes, training dogs) as part of their routine.

We run a school, where students come for religious instruction and to be certified as rabbis. We charge tuition for this service, which means that our students are, so to speak, our *customers*. They're paying for, and they deserve, our full attention. And we're not in some remote mountain hideaway in the Adirondacks, either. We're in Boca Raton, surrounded by golf courses and yacht clubs. The monks can raise dogs because they live apart — they are, as the saying goes, in the world but not of it. We're both in it and of it up to our eyeballs.

And so, between the sneezing and the wheezing and the itching of the eyes, I found myself wondering why, if there are dozens of seminaries and hundreds (if not thousands) of dog training schools around the country, did the two have to be brought together here?

Then, one day, I was teaching a course called God: Past, Present, and Future. And, as fate would have it, I opened the class by asking what the students thought God's love was. They all started to ponder the question, except Ms. Echo Silverstein, whose hand immediately shot up and who didn't wait to be called on to answer. "A dog's love is the same as God's love," she said. "That's why 'dog' is 'god' spelled backwards."

Well, naturally, I thought this was about the most jejune and ridiculous — and impious — thing I had ever heard. And so did the other students. A great shout of derision went up and I thought we were going to have a small riot on our hands.

But then a strange and very touching thing happened. One student, a Mr. Kyle Greenblatt, grudgingly admitted that Ms. Silverstein had a point. Mr. Greenblatt then went on to recount a story about the dog of his childhood years. And, one by one, everyone else shared their dog stories, too. By the end of the class we had spent ninety minutes not mentioning God once, but speaking, over and over, about love.

I must admit that I came away from that session deeply moved. In fact I would say that I was inspired. The similarity between what we hope for from God, and what we get without question from dogs, is too striking to be ignored. Isn't God's love that which makes us feel less alone and a little less afraid? And can we not say the same about the devotion of dogs? Doesn't God love us no matter what? And can we not say the same about dogs?

In the end, I had to agree. Echo was absolutely right. A dog's love is the same as God's love. In fact I would even go so far as to say that a dog's love teaches us something we don't always learn from God.

A dog teaches us *how to be loved.*

Dogs are able to do this because they sneak past our defenses and under all our walls of distraction, self-centeredness, sophistication, or what-have-you. They completely ignore our KEEP OUT signs and then, once they get in, they hit us with a tsunami of love. We like to think that dogs need us, but the truth is that we need them. They are there to share the good times and to comfort us through the bad. They'll offer up their cold wet noses on a hot summer day and share their warm bodies on a cold winter's night. They take us out of ourselves. They draw our attention to the here and now. They show us what it means to be patient, alert, focused, calm, nuts, vigilant, brave, kind, and curious.

All of which is to say, dogs make us better human beings — something of which I'm sure God would heartily approve. And so if you'll excuse me, I'm late for my shot.

— *Rabbi Paul*
Boca Raton, Florida

Acknowledgments

Lanmana Parys — For yeoman photography assisting both behind and in front of the camera; sensitive dog handling; and computer skills only someone born after the Reagan administration could be expected to possess

Samira Saha — For being a complete sweetheart while bringing and managing Deuce, the Miniature Pinscher Who Smirks

Coby Brown and Samy, Matt Brown and Willie, Brian Frazer and Nancy Cohen and Kenyon, and Amanda Mears-Duckett and Biscuit — For helping to make the Griffith Park/Rabbi shoot the exercise in chaos and absurdity it was meant to be

Terry Adams — For his usual astute editorship, canny comments, open-mindedness, and nimble avoidance of people with torches

Paul Bresnick — For stalwart agenting, unending enthusiasm, and sound strategizing

David Misch — For his patience and availability at not one but two sessions, in robes and with cats and everything, while simultaneously being completely amusing and a mensch

Erin Gallegos — For somehow being beautiful and graceful while pretending to brush her teeth and read, and for managing Copper, the Beagle with the Prehensile Nose

Kyle and Jennifer Parks — For the selfless and loving act that brought us the great (wonderful, gigantic) gift of Jaxon

Elizabeth Akers and Rhodesian Ridgeback Rescue of Northern California — For helping to bring Jax into our lives and for all of the work she does for rescue

Andrew Davilman — For being one of our biggest fans and supporters, both emotionally and spiritually

Andrew Kravchenko — For bringing Molly into our world and, by introducing us to ridgebacks, forever changing our lives

Allergy and Asthma Institute of the Valley — For the allergy shots that actually seem to be working

Zoe Braverman — For her lissome grace and model-like poise while loaded down with gear, and for bringing Bessie, who is as soulful as she is shaggy

Our mothers and our subsequent therapists (they know who they are), who encouraged us to use humor both to deal with life and themselves

And, of course —

Jaxon, Peaches, Blue, Deuce, Copper, and Bessie — For being their unique doggie selves

About the Authors

The Rabbis of the Boca Raton Theological Seminary are figments of the imagination of Ellis Weiner and Barbara Davilman, who live and write in Los Angeles and who, over the years, have applied the principles in this book to the care and feeding of many canine friends.

About the Photographer

Susan Burnstine is a fine art and commercial photographer living in Los Angeles with her dog, Blue.